THE MILFORD SERIES
POPULAR WRITERS OF TODAY
ISSN 0163-2469
VOLUME FIFTY-FOUR

Algebraic Fantasies and Realistic Romances

More Masters of Science Fiction

by

Brian Stableford

BORGO PRESS / WILDSIDE PRESS

www.wildsidepress.com

Library of Congress Cataloging-in-Publication Data

Stableford, Brian M.
    Algebraic fantasies and realistic romances : more masters of science fic-
tion / by Brian Stableford.
        p. cm. — (The Milford series. Popular writers of today, ISSN 0163-
2469 ; v. 54)
    Includes bibliographical references and index.
    ISBN 0-89370-183-1 (cloth). — ISBN 0-89370-283-8 (pbk.)
    1. Science fiction, English—History and criticism. 2. Science fiction,
American—History and criticism. 3. Fantastic fiction, English—History
and criticism. 4. English fiction—20th century—History and criticism. I.
Title. II. Series.
PR888.S35S72 1995   94-31347
823'.087609—dc20   CIP

SECOND PRINTING

CONTENTS

ABOUT BRIAN STABLEFORD

BRIAN MICHAEL STABLEFORD was born in Yorkshire in 1948. He taught at the University of Reading for many years, but is now a full-time writer. He has written many science-fiction and fantasy novels, most recently *The Empire of Fear*, *The Werewolves of London*, and *The Angel of Pain*. He has also contributed hundreds of biographical and critical articles to reference books on science fiction, fantasy, and horror, including both editions of *The Encyclopedia of Science Fiction*. His doctoral thesis was published in 1987 by Borgo Press as *The Sociology of Science Fiction*. Other Borgo Press publications by Stableford include: *Firefly: A Novel of the Far Future* (1994), *Masters of Science Fiction: Essays on Six Science Fiction Authors* (1981), *A Clash of Symbols: The Triumph of James Blish* (1979), and the forthcoming collection *Opening Minds: Essays on Fantastic Literature* (1995).

INTRODUCTION

Four of the essays in this collection were originally published in *Foundation*. "The Future Between the Wars: The Speculative Fiction of John Gloag," was in *Foundation* no. 20 (October 1980). The essay on Edgar Fawcett appeared as "The Realistic Romances of Edgar Fawcett" in *Foundation* no. 24 (February 1982). "The Politics of Evolution: Philosophical Themes in the Speculative Fiction of M. P. Shiel" was in *Foundation* no. 27 (February 1983), and was reprinted in *Shiel in Diverse Hands*, edited by A. Reynolds Morse (1983). "Animal Spirits: The Erotic and the Supernatural in Michael Jackson's *Thriller* Video" was in *Foundation* no. 35 (Winter, 1985).

"Algebraic Fantasies: The Science Fiction of Bob Shaw" was written for a pamphlet celebrating the author's work issued by the British Science Fiction Association, edited by Paul Kincaid and Geoff Rippington, and published in 1981. The remaining two articles were written for a series called "The Big Sellers," featured in the British SF magazine, *Interzone* (whose editor thought it a neat way of getting the names of best-selling authors on the cover even though they never submitted anything to the magazine). The article on Douglas Adams was in *Interzone* no. 30 (July/August 1989), and the piece on Stephen R. Donaldson in *Interzone* no. 32 (November/December 1989).

The articles on John Gloag and M. P. Shiel were both written while I was researching my book, *Scientific Romance in Britain, 1890-1950* (Fourth Estate, 1985). It was impossible, given the broad scope of that work, to give very detailed accounts of the work of the various authors covered therein, and I thought such consideration warranted in these cases because of the relative neglect of Gloag and the sometimes misleading nature of previous commentaries on Shiel's work. Like the essay on Edgar Fawcett, these works reflect my perennial fascination with obscure by-ways of the history of imaginative fiction—a fascination which led one not-entirely-unkind critic to describe me as "the world's foremost expert on books nobody has ever read by authors nobody has ever heard of." In more recent times I have made blatant attempts to compensate for this occasional esotericism with my contributions to "The Big Sellers" series, and my long series of articles on "Yesterday's Bestsellers" for the ill-fated *Million: The Magazine About Popular Fiction*; the article on Michael Jackson's *Thriller* video may be regarded as a further step in this direction. It is nowadays my fondest dream to be hired as a critic of Gothic rock music by some right-on publication with huge sales and cartloads of street cred; like most fond dreams, it is of course highly unlikely to come true.

I have not attempted to update any of the articles, save for altering some of the passages in the essay on John Gloag to take aboard the fact of his death soon after its publication; I thought it best to leave intact my critical impressions of the time at which each essay was written.

—Brian Stableford
Reading, England
19 September 1994

I.

THE FUTURE BETWEEN THE WARS

THE SPECULATIVE FICTION OF JOHN GLOAG

The first World War brought to an end a particular phase in the history of British speculative fiction. The economic pressures resulting from the war eroded the importance of the major medium in which speculative fiction had previously flourished: popular magazines like *The Strand, Pearson's Magazine*, and *The Idler*. The war was also responsible for considerable changes in attitudes to the future, which make the speculative fiction of the period between the wars distinct in its characteristic tone and its dominant concerns.

The decade of the Great War saw a marked change in the population of writers who were significant contributors to British speculative fiction. George Griffith died some years before the war began, and his last futuristic novel was published posthumously in 1911. William Hope Hodgson was killed in action. John Beresford and M. P. Shiel both abandoned speculative fiction for a considerable period in the twenties and thirties, though both returned to it briefly at the end of their careers. Sir Arthur Conan Doyle's interest in spiritualism reduced his literary output and carried him into less fertile imaginative territory. The pre-eminent figure in the history of British SF, H. G. Wells, virtually abandoned the kind of scientific romance which had helped make him famous, and his post-war speculative fiction consists mainly of fictionalized essays.

To compensate for this draining of resources, a new generation of writers emerged, most notable among them Olaf Stapledon and S. Fowler Wright. Excellent speculative fiction was also written by many other writers less specialized than these two in their output, including Aldous Huxley and George Bernard Shaw. Writers less well-known who made a significant contribution to the *genre* include Muriel Jaeger, E. C. Large, and John Gloag. The demise of *The Strand* and similar magazines meant that, in contrast to the pre-war writers, these writers wrote little short fiction and their novels were not serialized before book publication. Their books had less chance of finding a wide audience, and with the exception of Huxley's *Brave New World*, few of their works achieved any sudden success in their native land. Stapledon had to wait many years for his true status as a writer to be acknowledged, and some of his contemporaries still have not received the credit they deserve. John Gloag is one of them.

John Gloag was born in 1896. His first novel, published in 1932, was *Tomorrow's Yesterday*; this was followed in 1933 by *The New Pleasure* and in 1934 by *Winter's Youth*. His literary output during the thirties was very diverse, including numerous non-fiction works and contemporary novels. Two of his later novels are purely speculative—*Manna* (1940) and *99%* (1944)—and two others contain some speculative material: *Sacred Edifice* (1937) and *Slow* (1954). His short fiction, which includes a good deal of material written for broadcasting, includes a few

ALGEBRAIC FANTASIES & REALISTIC ROMANCES, by Brian Stableford

SF stories. His other work includes numerous books on architecture, design and furniture, and also works on social history. He was active as a writer until his death in 1981; his last works of fiction were historical novels set in Roman Britain: *Caesar of the Narrow Seas* (1969), *The Eagles Depart* (1973), and *Artorius Rex* (1977).

Before his death Mr. Gloag was kind enough to answer some questions regarding the speculative novels which he wrote in the thirties, and to provide me with some background information about his life. He was then the only British writer of speculative fiction active between the wars who was still alive to comment on the attitudes implicit in his fiction, and if there were no other reason, he would warrant investigation on that score alone. He was, however, one of the better writers of the period, and his speculative novels remain eminently readable today, despite the fact that the futures represented therein have dated. They are not much discussed in American reference books dealing with the history of speculative fiction, but this is because they have been overlooked—they will, in fact, amply reward consideration, both in terms of their historical significance as exemplars of the imaginative climate of their day, and in terms of their entertainment value.

I am greatly indebted to Mr. Gloag for allowing me to consult him and ask his opinion about the impressions I gained from reading his books, but the responsibility for any errors or distortions in the following essay is entirely mine.[1]

The most dramatic effect which the first world war had upon the characteristic attitudes expressed in futuristic fiction was, of course, upon the attitude to war itself. From 1871, when George Chesney published his account of "The Battle of Dorking" in order to alert the British public to the threat posed by German militarism, until 1914, when the war actually began, the most prolific species of futuristic fiction produced in Britain was the future war story. For the most part, these stories delighted in the contemplation of coming conflict—there is a persistent tendency in them to revel in the excitement of war and to look forward with chauvinistic enthusiasm to the day when Britain might demonstrate to the rest of the world the true extent of her moral and military supremacy.

The man whose novels in this vein may be regarded as archetypal is William Le Queux, author of *The Invasion of 1910*, whose serialization in the *Daily Mail* during 1906 was turned into a mammoth publicity stunt by the paper's proprietor, Alfred Harmsworth (later Lord Northcliffe). Many popular writers contributed to the species, including Louis Tracy (*The Final War*, 1896), Max Pemberton (*Pro Patria*, 1901), and Edgar Wallace (*Private Selby*, 1912), while two writers who built their earlier reputations on works in this vein were George Griffith (*The Angel of the Revolution*, 1893) and M. P. Shiel (*The Yellow Danger*, 1899).

Though many of these writers—most notably Griffith and Shiel—foresaw bloodshed on a colossal scale as a result of advances in military technology, they tended to contemplate the prospect with relish. A more cautious approach is evident in Erskine Childers's *The Riddle of the Sands* (1903) and C. J. Cutcliffe Hyne's *Empire of the World* (1910), but there were few others whose main concern was the possibility of avoiding war rather than indulging in it. Even H. G. Wells, who not only realized that the scale of destruction featured in the next war might be far greater than in any previous conflict, but also appreciated the tragic implications of that fact, was ambivalent in his attitude because of his conviction that the present social order must be torn down if it was to be replaced by a better one. Both *The War in the Air* (1908) and *The World Set Free* (1914) provide eloquent testimony to this ambivalence.

8

Once the Great War had ended, however, this optimism was lost. Trench warfare in France drained the credibility from notions of the magnificence and glorious excitement of war, and implanted a horror and disgust that grew as the truth filtered through the web of propaganda which temporarily confined it. The disillusionment suffered first by the fighting men and later by the British public is elegantly expressed by R. C. Sherriff's successful play, *Journey's End*, which opened in 1929. Wells's hope that the tragedy might be ameliorated by the reordering of international relations and progress toward a World State quickly evaporated. His optimistic essay on the proposals for the formation of a League of Nations, *In the Fourth Year: Anticipations of a World Peace* (1918) was followed not long after by *The Salvaging of Civilization*, which declares that

> ...unless the ever more violent and disastrous incidence of war can be averted, unless some common controls can be imposed on the headlong waste of man's limited inheritance of coal, oil and moral energy that is now going on, the history of humanity must presently culminate in some sort of disaster, repeating and exaggerating the disaster of the great war, producing chaotic social conditions, and going on thereafter in a degenerative process towards extinction.

This attitude, as might be expected, is widely represented in the futuristic fiction of the twenties. *The People of the Ruins* (1920) by Edward Shanks has its protagonist delivered into the next century *via* suspended animation, and there he finds civilization in collapse and England reverted to barbarism. The knowledge he possesses might be extremely valuable in this world that has lost its history and its intellectual heritage, but his host is only interested in his knowledge of artillery; and he has no option but to take part in yet another conflict whose result is further degeneration. Similar images recur frequently, in such works as Cicely Hamilton's *Theodore Savage* (1922, revised as *Lest Ye Die*); P. A. Graham's *The Collapse of Homo Sapiens* (1923); Shaw Desmond's *Ragnarok* (1926), and John Collier's *Tom's a-Cold* (1933, known in the U.S. as *Full Circle*). To the horror of war itself was added a sense of the *vulnerability* of civilization.

John Gloag was one of the few important writers of speculative fiction who was on active service during the Great War, and he comments on his experiences as follows:

> I served in the Welsh Guards during the latter part of the 1914-18 War, and was in France (as a subaltern) on the Western Front with the first battalion of my regiment and took part in the big push that smashed into the Hindenburg Line in August 1918, when I collected some lungfuls of poison gas (our own chiefly, for we were far ahead of our barrage in the attack when I was knocked out), and was invalided home. It's necessary to tell you all this, as what I experienced in the army and on active service had a profound effect upon my imagination, and to some extent coloured my fiction when I wrote short stories and novels after the Great War. (Engraved on one of the routine medals I collected, suspended from what was known as "the Victory ribbon," are the words: "the Great War for Civilisation." That's a laugh, in view of the sort of civilisation we've had ever since!)

Gloag directed a good deal of serious thought to the question of the vulnerability of modern society to the effects of disaster. One of his earliest published works was the essay, *Artifex; or, The Future of Craftsmanship* (1926), which was published as part of the influential series of speculative pamphlets known as the *Today & Tomorrow* series (1924-30). He introduces his subject as follows:

> Many writers have brought their critical and imaginative gifts to picturing the condition of civilization in the future, fifty, a hundred, or two hundred years hence. Some of these studies in futurity have been presented as fiction, and if we glance at the most pessimistic forecasts we realize with something of a shock how absolutely dependent we are for our present security and comfort upon the skill, individual and co-ordinated, of craftsmen, the people who actually make things or assist in the production of scores of our everyday articles—pots and pans, needles, thimbles, shoes, glass, tobacco-pipes, and a thousand and one objects we accept without much thought concerning the way they were made.[2]

He goes on to summarize the theme of *People of the Ruins* and *Theodore Savage* (he also quotes from *The War in the Air* and mentions Jack London's story of a depopulated world, "The Scarlet Plague") and adds the judgment that:

> The books referred to are not just stories to be dismissed as such after a few shudders by way of tribute to the authors' ability in creating an atmosphere of horror. They should be recognized as thoughtful comments on very real and highly unpleasant possibilities.[3]

He goes on from there to attempt to analyze and answer the question of whether modern society could, indeed, suffer such a reverse as to find itself without the necessary resources of efficient craftsmanship. The main body of the essay is concerned with examining the relationship between modern manufacturing methods and the skill of craftsmen, and the effect of mass production upon the potential for artistry in design. The conclusion is careful and optimistic, but the introduction offers eloquent testimony to an undercurrent of anxiety. It is not surprising that when he began to turn his hand to the writing of fiction Gloag chose to produce a futuristic fantasy echoing those which had earlier stimulated his imagination, though by no means simply replicating their images.

Tomorrow's Yesterday is, first and foremost, a novel which arises out of a particular climate of thought, and reflects a view of the world appropriate to it. It is worth noting, though, that it is also a work which belongs to an authentic literary tradition. It is easy to overlook the fact that a coherent tradition of speculative fiction quite independent of the one which grew up in America around the science fiction magazines existed in parallel in Britain. There is a series of writers, headed by the enormously influential figure of Wells, who were aware of one another's activities, and aware, too, of some degree of common inspiration and common cause. As well as the writers cited, Gloag read S. Fowler Wright, and remembers the futuristic fiction of Kipling and Huxley. He named Olaf Stapledon as "a valued friend...with whom I used to have stimulating discussions about imaginary worlds." The close connection which existed in Britain between speculative fiction and speculative nonfiction is emphasized by his involvement with the *Today & Tomorrow* series (other *Today & Tomorrow* essayists who also wrote futuristic fiction include André Maurois, Robert Graves, Bertrand Russell, Muriel Jaeger, A. M. Low, H. F. Heard, and J. B. S. Haldane), and by his enthusiastic recommendation of Haldane's *Possible Worlds*.

Tomorrow's Yesterday was originally conceived as a film script, and the script itself occupies a little over half its text, bracketed by several chapters of narrative. In the book, the film becomes a production put on by the mysterious New Century Theatre. The story reflects most of the author's interests of the day—at this time he was building up his own advertising agency as well as writing—and is primarily concerned with the advertising campaign which heralds the opening of the new theatre (an architectural marvel), and with the critical reception of the production.

The film (in three-dimensional color projection!) concerns the observations made by two humanold creatures trying to analyze and understand the historical fate of the species which they have replaced: *Homo sapiens*. The opening scenes present a satirical account of the role of the sexual impulse in human affairs, and of its exploitation by advertising; the later ones describe the advent of a destructive war and the subsequent gradual reversion of humankind to savagery. In the last stages of decadence, savage humans worship the wheel—a symbol of almost-forgotten greatness which has become the object of human sacrifices intended to placate the gods and stave off disaster. It transpires that all is not quite lost, for the observers (who have evolved from cats) bring out of the past a human sociologist and explain to him that he is the first of many. They tell him that:

> As our kind developed their brains they conquered fear and lust, for the first scientists soon learned to mechanize the reproductive processes, so that in half a million years sex was altogether silenced, leaving us a freedom men had never known. We concentrated on the conquest of every problem that science discovered, and we are still only in the beginning of knowledge, even though we have colonies in the stars and have ranged back in time and found, what some of our early biologists suspected, that there had been a strange experiment in civilization before ours—the experiment of man. This experiment will serve us and our world, for, as we told you, we shall draw from that past of man the great minds that rose above their kind and tried to reach and make things that would endure. Of these, you are the first, and we chanced upon you in our first visits to the world you knew. You will help us to bring back all the wasted wisdom of man to the life of the world, and great men shall live again.[4]

The sociologist, however, suspects that the great men, embittered by what they will learn of the fate of their race, might prefer oblivion to the prospect of re-creation by courtesy of another race. This question is left open, to be further dramatized by the response of the public to the spectacle placed before it. The film itself is satirical, but the surrounding material is doubly so—the audience is beyond the reach of the message which the film is trying to get across, resentful letters appear in the papers following an almost unanimously hostile response from the critics. There seems to be no future for the New Century Theatre, and no sooner has it announced the title of its next production, *War Gods Wake*, than it is forced to close because of a state of national emergency...

11

The principal reason why *Tomorrow's Yesterday* stands out among contemporary speculative novels is its tone. Though it is in some respects a recognizably Wellsian work (Wells had produced his own "book of a film," *The King Who Was a King*, in 1929) its ironic quality is very much Gloag's own. Sharp satire was one of the few things that Wells was not very good at, and his most heavily sarcastic works—*Boon* and *The Camford Visitation* are the best examples—are rather ponderous and unsubtle. *Tomorrow's Yesterday* contrives to be scathing while retaining the finesse and lightness of touch essential to successful satire.

In fact, this satirical approach was something rarely seen in British speculative fiction, especially in connection with so serious a theme. Wells advanced the view that the best way to write scientific romance was to import single innovative hypotheses into narratives which were otherwise carefully realistic—only thus, he supposed, could the new ideas possibly be taken seriously. The growing familiarity of futuristic scenarios permitted some relaxation of this rule, but even so *Tomorrow's Yesterday* stands out as a boldly innovative work. It is similar in several ways to the satires and black comedies that began to appear in American SF of the fifties, principally in *Galaxy*. The only contemporary speculative work which is as sharp in its ironic treatment of serious matters is *The Spacious Adventures of the Man in the Street* (1928) by the Irish satirist Eimar O'Duffy, which is much less focused and contains a good deal of pure comedy. There are several Utopian satires of the period, but nothing that deals with anything as deadly serious as the threat of apocalyptic war. It is not until we look at the last twenty years, when science fiction writers began the prolific production of mocking tales of the self-destruction of civilization *via* overpopulation and pollution, that we can find a more accurate parallel.

Gloag's second novel, *The New Pleasure*, shows the same ironic finesse and delicacy of touch as *Tomorrow's Yesterday*, but to rather different purpose. Its theme is not the destruction of civilization, but its salvation—or, rather, the salvation of humankind from the more awful aspects of civilization. The agent of this change is as different as can be from the wars which Wells used to smash up the old world order in *The War in the Air* and *The World Set Free*; but it is very different too from the miraculous alternatives which Wells produced in *In the Days of the Comet* and *The Autocracy of Mr. Parham*, which are based on a rather curious theory of moral chemistry. Gloag's agent of change is ingenious and imaginatively appealing in comparison.

The story begins with the invention of a drug code-named Gamma-8 and subsequently marketed under the name "Voe." It is the imaginative counterpart of a local anaesthetic—a restricted stimulant which selectively affects the sense of smell, at the same time producing a pleasurable, euphoric sensation. The plot of the novel follows the fight to market the drug against the opposition of various vested interests (principally the tobacco industry), and the effect which the ultimate habituation of the British public to its use has upon their way of life.

It transpires that tobacco is only one of the obnoxious things which has been tolerated in the human environment only because men have hitherto existed in a state of olfactory anaesthesia. Petrol fumes are equally intolerable, and so are most cosmetics and lack of personal hygiene. A new age of discretion dawns as men become capable of realizing to the full which aspects of modern life, in a literal *and* metaphorical sense, stink. Their awakened noses lead them to a new promised land, leading to much greater discrimination even in sexual relationships, promoting an entirely natural eugenic selection that reduces the population greatly. As the inventor of Voe, Adrian Frankby (canonized by future generations as St. Adrian), travels up the Thames in the closing chapters, he reflects that the new England he has been instrumental in creating would resemble the picture painted by William Morris in *News from Nowhere*, were it not for the fact that the architecture of *this* new world is so much more magnificent.

The New Pleasure provides one of the most stylish and charming prospectuses for social salvation ever written. Its satirical tone is much more gentle than that of *Tomorrow's Yesterday*, and the work has a flavor which is quite unique. Like *Tomorrow's Yesterday*, it finds a faint resonance in recent American science fiction, but whereas recent apocalyptic fantasies frequently recapitulate the mocking irony of Gloag's first novel, recent stories of tactical retreat from the uglier aspects of technology are usually deadly serious, lightened only by a curious quasi-religious "ecological mysticism." There is a sense in which *The New Pleasure* is still ahead of the time which can produce such novels as Ernest Callenbach's *Ecotopia*, for it includes within the scope of its irony exactly such lyrical celebrations of the re-establishment of harmony with nature. The final chapter of the book describes the unveiling of a statue of St. Adrian which is to encapsulate the spirit of the salvation which he brought to mankind:

> It was a naked figure. The right hand was raised to the nose, with the forefinger and thumb touching the nostrils as though conveying a pinch of Voe. The left hand was stretched aloft with the index finger pointing to the sky, for the sculptor had resisted the inspiration of the cartoon-symbolist school, which would have compelled him to put in the figure's right hand a sword with a bowler hat impaled thereon, thus relegating to the left hand the vital Voe-taking gesture.[5]

Beneath the charm and humor, however, there remains a serious note of disenchantment with the quality of contemporary civilization and culture. This reaction against certain contemporary trends and fashions mingles in Gloag's work with the intimations of cultural mortality which constantly invade it. It is striking that what all of his central characters have in common is an urge to *withdraw* into a secure private enclave where they can be safe and comfortable—a feeling which seems to sit uneasily alongside the strong sense of duty and concern for their fellow men which they also share. When they are called upon to do their bit, they do so wholeheartedly (though sometimes pessimistically), but they always look forward to the time when they can retire from the fray in order to follow their private and idiosyncratic concerns. This is true of Adrian Frankby in *The New Pleasure*, more so of Lord Privilege in *Winter's Youth*, and even more so of Jacob Drune in *Sacred Edifice*. This correlates with a sense of disconnection from the world's affairs which seems evident in the world-view of several notable writers of speculative fiction (John Beresford and S. Fowler Wright provide the most striking examples among Gloag's contemporaries). The central characters of Gloag's later novels become steadily more disenchanted with the worlds in which they find themselves, particularly as their fashions are exemplified by the ambitions and attitudes of the younger characters who provide them with dramatic counterpoints. *99%* is a novel positively saturated by disenchantment.

The roots of this disenchantment clearly originate in the disillusionment of the Great War, but its growth was nourished by other historical trends. When *The New Pleasure* was written, this steady growth had hardly begun—the disenchantment of the novel reflects nothing more than the evaporation of the myth of material progress toward a technological Utopia. In the year that it was published, however,

Adolf Hitler became Chancellor of Germany, and the rise of Nazism began to provide further cause for alarm. The specter of Hitler—the ghost of horrors yet to come—lurks in the background of all Gloag's subsequent speculative novels, and appears to have driven away the spirit of innocent amusement that makes *The New Pleasure* so seductive.

Winter's Youth extends arguments contained in the first two novels, and adds more. It is basically a political satire set in the 1960s, and there are some aspects of it that faintly echo the humorous political fantasies of Hilaire Belloc. The theme connecting the elements of the plot is the determination of the Second National Government to hold on to power and popularity by whatever means become available. After a disastrous public relations exercise connected with the promotion of a supposed new gospel which turns out to be a fake, the cabinet elects to take credit for sponsoring a rejuvenation process discovered by one Dr. Nordelf. This move turns out to be mistaken, leading to extreme discontent among the young, and the founding of a new opposition party, the Social Revivalists, which stands a far better chance of taking power than the old opposition party, the Communist-Fascists. The rejuvenated cabinet hangs on desperately, but its excessive self-interest and advancing senility eventually leads the nation into a series of calamities culminating in the three days war, in which four million people die.

The observer who provides the commentary on this sequence of events is Lord Privilege, a descendant of Captain Marryat's Peter Simple and the one clear-sighted man in the ill-fated cabinet, where he serves as foreign secretary. His mission in life is to preserve Europe from the horror of war—a horror which has increased considerably since the invention of "radiant inflammatol," a weapon powerful enough to obliterate whole cities. There being no defense against radiant inflammatol, it has become a kind of ultimate deterrent, with no nation daring to provoke its use; but Lord Privilege knows that in spite of this he is trying to preserve a situation which must, in the long run, deteriorate. His sense of detachment from the complex pattern of events is greatly enhanced by his acceptance of the fact that things are, in the final analysis, outside his control. He is perhaps the most interesting character in any of Gloag's novels, for his fatalism is unusually complicated, tempered by compassion for others, a strong sense of irony, and a gentle undercurrent of hedonism.

Winter's Youth is a more sober novel than its predecessors; its ironies are deliberately understated. The way in which the Nordelf process becomes part of everyday life is unmelodramatic, and so is the process of a concomitant plot by the British Medical Association to use its gifts for a little covert eugenic selection. One of the side-effects of the process is to inculcate in its beneficiaries a rather perverted interest in sadism and debauchery, but this too is domesticated into more-or-less harmless ritual. Even the war is passed over in an interlude between chapters, and the reader learns about it as it is filtered into the stream of Lord Privilege's memories, denuded of its terrible significance. The climax of the story is anything but apocalyptic, dealing with the quiet passing away of the one man who preferred to let nature take its course and refused to submit to the indignity of the Nordelf process. The casual acceptance of events such as these as part and parcel of the everyday affairs of twentieth-century man has a greater impact than impassioned rhetoric could have. The occasional moments of vitriolic cynicism are all the more powerful because of this setting.

One of the key judgments passed by Lord Privilege is contained in the comments which he makes regarding one of the "fevered orgies" conducted by his Nordelfized colleagues, where the author observes that:

> Lord Privilege knew enough about history and humanity to understand that religious teaching always rotted down into ritual; for the mob demanded ritual: truth was too bleak for the common mind; it pulled away the layers of belief that, piled up like eiderdowns on a bed, kept thought comfortably drowsy. He knew that most mid-twentieth century Europeans had lost their religious convictions without losing their taste for ritual. Only intelligent men could bear the isolation and spiritual responsibility of scepticism. Orthodox religions had become spiritually unrefreshing symbols of social standing, except in Germany, where the new paganism was fiercely alive; but in the Christian countries of Europe and America the revival of strange cults, secret societies with private rituals of their own, and of magic, witchcraft and witch covens, was a symptom of the unacknowledged and largely unrecognized loss of connection between the life of the body and the needs of the soul.[6]

This diagnosis of our contemporary predicament sounds quite familiar to our ears, perhaps because we have seen so many more of the symptoms which Gloag anticipated. (It should be remembered that the passage quoted was written nearly twenty years before Gerald Gardner popularized "witch covens" as a modish form of lifestyle fantasy.) The characterization of Lord Privilege's detachment as "the isolation and spiritual responsibility of scepticism" is particularly interesting, for it is exactly Gloag's charge against his contemporaries that they were all-too-often lacking in spiritual responsibility, ever-ready to seize upon new dogmas and to be betrayed by them.

When Privilege observes the deterioration of his country's affairs under the Nordelfized cabinet, this is the observation which he makes:

> If this type of preliminary decay, this mental enervation, was affecting the ruling classes in other countries some peculiar things might occur. Was the world really coming under the direction of minds that were half in ruins? Even if it was, his habitual skepticism inclined him to doubt whether mankind's affairs would be conducted very differently. A mad tyrant like Caligula or Nero was often only the equivalent of a government of elected professional politicians. Intentional malignancy and injustice could be directly attributed to a tyrant; he was a convenient figurehead for a nation's wrongs; but only stupidity or well-meaning incompetence could be attributed to a political party when misery and injustice endured under its power.[7]

This is the political predicament which is corollary to the spiritual predicament indicated by Privilege in the earlier passage; on the one hand waits the evil of tyranny, on the other the treachery of stupidity, and the attempt to steer a course between them is bedevilled by many difficulties. The attractiveness of political substitutes for religion—Militarism, Fascism and Marxism, in particular—is represented in Gloag's books as a crucial, and potentially fatal, failure of scepticism and renunciation of spiritual responsibility. In this regard too the author's rhetoric still seems forceful to the reader of today.

ALGEBRAIC FANTASIES & REALISTIC ROMANCES, by Brian Stableford

Winter's Youth can be seen as a kind of summing up of the attitudes and arguments evident in Gloag's early speculative fiction. Though his literary output continued to be prolific, he wrote no more futuristic fantasies for a while. His next novels were the thrillers *Sweet Racket* and *Ripe for Development*. It was in this period that he became extensively involved with broadcasting, and he wrote many short stories for the radio. (He also appeared frequently on the *Brains Trust* and other discussion programs, where his flair for ironic rhetoric must have served very well.) Because of the influence of the radio medium on his work, all of his short stories are brief and economical, and they are contructed so as to favor some kind of surprise revelation in the last line; they are designed to be *told* rather than to be read. Some are science fiction, but these were among the ones which were *not* broadcast, according to the indications given in the contents pages of his first collection, *It Makes a Nice Change* (1938).

"Pendulum," first published in the *London Mercury*, is an account of a vision experienced by a man injured in a car crash. Detached from his body, his consciousness begins to swing back and forth through time, to observe London in the distant past and far future, time and time again until some kind of "temporal friction" slows him down and brings him to rest inside his body once more. The point of the story is that as he swings in both "directions" he sees similar changes overtaking the city—no matter whether he is travelling forward or back in time he still sees the city slowly vanishing into forest and men degenerating into savages.

The same theme recurs in "The Slit," a Wellsian vignette in which the protagonist, visiting a friend who is a scientist, is offered an opportunity to use a machine which can look through time. He elects to look back at England in the fifth century, when the Dark Ages were closing in upon a land from which the guiding hand of Roman Empire had been recently withdrawn. What he sees he interprets in this light, and is horrified to learn afterwards that owing to a fault in the apparatus he has actually been looking into the future, at the England of the late twenty-first century.

Both of these stories are necessarily cursory in their treatment of this notion of historical cyclicity, but more depth was given to it when Gloag used it a third time, in the novel *Sacred Edifice*. Though this is primarily a contemporary novel, an added significance is lent to its events by the bracketing of the main narrative with scenes set in the distant past and far future—which prove, of course, to be strikingly similar.

The plot of the novel concerns the rebuilding of a storm-damaged Gothic cathedral, with the aid of a generous gift from an American millionaire. The architect who wins the commission to rebuild it is determined in some way to recapitulate the endeavor of the original builders, who attempted to incarnate in its architecture the spirit of their religion. Rather than simply restoring it, he wants to build a sacred edifice adequate to the twentieth century: one which will perform a parallel socio-psychological function for the modern men and women who will worship in it. This feat he eventually accomplishes.

This is an unusual theme for a novel, and only a man with Gloag's unusual combination of interests and abilities could have planned and executed it. (He reports that "it was conceived as a complete story during a visit to the fragment of the abbey church at Malmesbury when my wife and I were wandering about the west country in our car in the summer of 1936. Within hours, I seem to recollect, the tale of the great church of Brell—my imagined sacred edifice—was unfolded, peopled with characters, though of course the chief character is the great building itself.")

The main narrative is fascinating in itself, and the interaction of the characters is handled delicately and effectively, but the depth of vision added by the extended temporal perspective provides a whole new dimension. The story of the rebuilding and regeneration of the cathedral has its immediate historical context—that of the depression and the threat to world peace posed by Nazi Germany—but this context too takes its place in an immensely wider perspective provided by the vision of Kara, a stone-age priest who selects the site ultimately to be occupied by the church as the place where his own sacred edifice (a stone circle) properly belongs. His vision foresees the building and rebuilding of the Gothic cathedral, but also reveals the fate of the architect's dream, which proves (inevitably) to be as frail in substance and as transient in meaning as its predecessor:

> Kara could see the gaunt ruins of the cathedral; the medieval stonework of the nave and chancel still faithfully upholding the roof; but from the wreck of the central tower and transepts, rusty steel girders emerged like blood-stained bones from powdering concrete. The city on the hillside had almost disappeared. Dimpled mounds covered with coarse grass entombed its houses. On the crest of the downs a few huts were grouped behind earthen ramparts, and on the site where Kara had marked out the first temples a circle of well-grown oaks surrounded a crude shrine, a cruciform roofless structure built from ragged pieces of concrete and large stones.
> Men still worshipped although half their lives were spent in secret lairs hiding from roving brigand bands. They lived in a lawless land of fear and magic, perplexed by legends of peace and order and plenty that their fathers, and grandfathers and great-grandfathers had handed down from some unimaginable golden age. In due time they would build again, and give praise to God with their skill. The work of building would drink up the love and understanding of a thousand lives until some sacred edifice should again challenge the sky with towers and resist the southwest wind that freshens the land men once called England.[8]

Sacred Edifice is very different from the two short stories "Pendulum" and "The Slit" in that the character who experiences the vision connecting past and future is situated outside the plot. His visions have been "tapped" by one of the deans of the cathedral who has written a history of the site which his successor considers overly imaginative, but they do not otherwise intrude. The perspective which the author adds *via* Kara's visions is a remote one—a "God's eye view" not altogether dissimilar to that frequently employed by Olaf Stapledon in his own attempts to place modern man in a much greater context.

The agent of destruction which reduces England (and presumably civilization as a whole) to ruins in these stories is, of course, war, and by the time that *Sacred Edifice* was written that war was looming on the horizon. The contemporary narrative ends with the mobilization of the European nations. The imminence of war seems to have been the primary force generating the persistent recurrence within Gloag's work of the kind of image described above. In one of his letters he states quite bluntly:

> My preoccupation with the future during the 1930s was generated (if you can generate a preoccupation) by the mounting hor-

ror of what was then the present, with a certifiable lunatic in charge of the most aggressive military nation in Europe.

As history turned out, Gloag's next futuristic novel was overtaken by events while it was in press. *Manna* was written in 1939, and the proofs were passed mere weeks before Hitler invaded Poland. By the time the book was published, in 1940, Europe was at war, as the novel's climax had predicted. It is the story of a conspiracy mounted by a group of influential men brought together after having been featured in a book of biographies written by a retired journalist. The journalist is the narrator of the book, though he only becomes involved in the conspiracy when he tries to find the cause of his book's suppression by its subjects.

One of the conspirators has developed a new kind of mushroom which will grow almost anywhere, and which provides all the nourishment that men need. Once released into the environment it can spread of its own accord, and if properly managed can banish forever the danger of hunger and the possibility of starvation. There are, however, two problems which need to be faced before mankind can be given this new manna. The first problem is to assure that society can readjust itself to circumstances in which the foremost of the Malthusian checks on population growth has been removed. The second, and more complex, problem is that the fungus has a side-effect not unlike that of the drug featured in *The New Pleasure*—it promotes tranquillity. One of the men in charge of the project suggests to the narrator that introducing manna to the contemporary scene would be "like introducing alcohol to a community of clean-living Polynesians." Such a gift, it is argued, might lead to the end of progress and the loss of initiative, and the last thing the conspirators want is to turn mankind into a race of lotus-eaters.

The narrator sees in manna tremendous potential for good, but in the course of the plot he becomes gradually disenchanted with most of the men whose biographies he had assembled under the title *Possible Rulers*. The implication is that if even *they* have feet of clay, what of the rest? Indeed, the reaction of most of the people who find out about manna is a hostile one. The narrator's son is a Marxist, and argues that science can never solve the problems of mankind, and that the amelioration of conflict between social classes by the introduction of a new opium into social affairs would be a catastrophe in its own right. The narrator cannot agree, but is made anxious by doubts that eventually crystallize as Europe lurches into war. With Hitler to be defeated, the possible effects of manna on the fighting forces become an ironic threat. The world's reception of this great gift is finally summed up by the Prime Minister in a broadcast to the nation:

> But there are more threats to the welfare of this nation, and indeed to the well-being of mankind, than those arising from political differences with our neighbours. Nature sometimes takes it upon herself to test the frailty of her creatures, and sometimes the test takes the form of a plague; sometimes it takes the form of a gift; an embarrassing gift. We have known occasions in the past when the bountiful hands of Nature have, by furnishing an indiscriminate plenty, nearly overset the delicately balanced economic machine of modern civilization. I should not conceal from you the fact that we are facing a very grave crisis, far graver than those political and international crises which have disfigured the history of this century.
> We are facing Nature, when Nature is in a mischievous mood. We have all heard of a growth, of a new plant, that has surged

over this country like a tidal wave. That plant has been impiously likened to the manna that fell from heaven upon the Israelites wandering in the wilderness. But...this is no gift from God; this so-called manna is a temptation of the devil...

The Government...must take steps against this plague, for plague it is. It is sapping the fine character of our people. It is as pernicious as opium. It is rotting that independence of outlook, destroying that individual integrity, and debilitating that reverence for immemorial institutions without which no country, and certainly no great empire, can long endure....This growth—this so-called food, this manna—must be destroyed, uprooted, burned out, seared from the surface of our fair land. The eating of manna will become an offence under the Law. Only by recognizing the evil that it may create and maintain can we have the courage to preserve our economic system and our great civilization.[9]

Here the story ends—as, in fact, it must. The kind of novel of the future which Gloag had been writing was rendered impotent by the onset of actual conflict. The catastrophe had arrived, and the attempt to plan for a better future was short-circuited and reduced to a final terse comment, the last section of the book, which simply reads:

Manna awaits the world. Will men have the wisdom and the courage to use it?[10]

It was a question that could not be asked again until peace was renewed. Indeed, it could not be asked again until people were once again *confident* of peace. John Gloag, at least, put aside this question and others like it for all time; after 1945 he wrote no more futuristic fantasies at all.

Gloag wrote one more speculative novel during the war: *99%*. Though it is not a futuristic work it recapitulates the theme of "Pendulum," "The Slit," and *Sacred Edifice*. The story follows the course of an experiment in which a number of individuals are "sent back in time" while they are asleep and dreaming, in order to re-live some moment of extreme significance experienced by one of their ancestors and transmitted through the generations by some kind of genetic memory. The several sub-plots of the story, as might be expected, focus on the various effects which the visions have on the lives of the protagonists. Each one finds himself rudely jolted out of his complacency, inspired to take a new and more dynamic approach to his affairs.

In the early chapters, the story appears to be more straightforward than in fact it is. A false trail laid by the author suggests that each participant in the experiment will burst through the imaginative bounds that confine him, and with the aid of whatever vital insight he has achieved will constructively remake his own life, possibly to the benefit of the world at large. The idea is attractive enough, and represents a moral sometimes advanced by similar stories—that if we could only break out of the confines of our mental prisons the revelation of the way of the world that would ensue could only be beneficial. However, Gloag's story is more subtle and rather more pessimistic than that, for although his characters readily seize upon this belief, all of them are betrayed by it in some measure. The world, unfortunately, proves to be singularly intractable in the face of their new fervor.

The most cruel of these exemplary narratives is that of the M.P. Carnaby Riggs, whose dream takes him back to experience the flight of a small boy from Carthage before its destruction by the Romans. The boy's father is a rich merchant, who produces a flow of cynical rhetoric regarding the virtues of opportunism and the politics of expediency. The merchant is optimistic, believing that when the present political troubles have blown over the world he knows will be restored to him. His lack of imagination is conclusively demonstrated when he is taken by slavers who murder him, appropriate all his goods, and take the boy to be sold.

Riggs cannot help but see the present in this long-lost past, and is appalled by this newly-revealed consistency in human affairs. He abandons his political career in favor of a messianic enthusiasm for Utopian regeneration, which takes him to Russia in search of the possibility of a new and better world. Alas, the reality of Russia cannot measure up to his inspiration, and conditions in the new world drive both himself and his wife to an early grave.

The judgments passed upon the other characters are less harsh, but even the man who actually learns most from his experience, and seems to have found some essential core of truth, can only react to his lesson by turning away from his life of more-or-less idle luxury to take up an ascetic and eremitic existence. (This eventuality is one which Schopenhauer would have approved of wholeheartedly, but it is much more appropriate than genuinely convincing.)

This particular experience allows Sir Stephen Trobell, a marine engineer with an exceptionally snobbish wife, temporarily to share the consciousness of a stone-age cave-dweller—a priest and visionary, like Kara of *Sacred Edifice*. By this means he is witness to a religious ritual in which the savages dance themselves to exhaustion, and which climaxes as follows:

> The women danced longer than the men of the tribe, but for two hours after the last woman had sunk down to earth in utter exhaustion, the priests continued whirling about the blackened ashes of their fire. Then, one by one, they dropped down, unconscious, until Af was left alone, spinning away from his body, away from the world as he knew it, leaving behind the tribes and the caves and the hunting grounds; leaving the kindly, sheltering spirit of the tribe, and adventuring alone, to gain the knowledge of things as they are.
>
> Of his own physical collapse, he knew nothing; for he was drawn away from his body, and his own mind merged into something far greater than the mind of a tribal priest. He saw the mind of mankind, growing and contracting; he saw it moving brightly towards light and glittering shapes, and returning, darkened, shrunken and scattered. It was like a luminous cloud; occasionally particles of it were detached, grew promisingly and vividly, and then broke up into innumerable fresh particles that sometimes expanded and flourished, but more often faded and blackened.
>
> He saw *through* the cloud, to an earth, green with vegetation, grey with water, belted and banded with golden deserts, and studded with white-tipped mountains. Everywhere on that varied stage pictures were forming and re-forming. Tribes came out of caves and roamed the forests, and then gave up hunting, and settled down to grow their food. Like an enormous panorama, he saw the spread of human life through the world. He observed the invention of building and the control of shelter changing the ways

and thoughts of men, and from huts and hovels, came houses, palaces, great monuments, cities, roads, machines, and a world full of movement. And everywhere, men became strangers to each other, and the luminous cloud of the world mind was attenuated, until only a few wisps of its filmy radiance survived. Men built and destroyed, generation after generation, until at last they built only for destruction, and whole tribes and continents gave their lives and dedicated their arts, to the making of machines that would burn and tear down what they had inherited from the past.[11]

And then, of course, the pattern is reversed, and mankind reverts to savagery and the worship of the wheel. New hunters emerge in order to re-establish the superiority of men over wild beasts, and new tribes form and expand until:

The mind of mankind began to glow once more, to coalesce, and through the iridescent mist a picture formed, of a figure with a white-painted face and mutilated hands, lying naked and unconscious across the ashes of a little fire, while rain beat down, and a concourse of people stood, silent and expectant.[12]

Af cannot tell his people about his vision, because he has not the words to convey its meaning. Trobell finds himself no better placed than the stone-age priest, and he finds no alternative but to retreat into quietism—an extreme form of the withdrawal that all Gloag's heroes find ultimately convenient.

The conclusion of *99%* is not so very different from the conclusion of *Tomorrow's Yesterday*, save for the addition of a little Stapledonian mysticism and the fact that mankind lives to rise again rather than being replaced by another species. The tone of the later book, however, is markedly different. The sharp satire is gone, replaced with a more ruthless and less amiable iconoclasm. The enormity of fate's cruelty is increased beyond the measure suggested in *Sacred Edifice*. Nevertheless, it is not a wholly pessimistic book, and the characters fortunate enough not to have shared Trobell's vision contrive to continue their lives with stout enough hearts. The book is bleakly bitter in what its vision suggests: that civilization is ephemeral; that enlightenment will not save us despite the fact that it is not illusory; that the spirit of man is valiant in adversity but cannot liberate itself from the frailty of the flesh. However, the author clearly recognizes the imperatives of the proximate reality as well as the inhumanity of infinity and eternity, and he recognizes that there are virtues as well as faults in its staunch resistance to the transforming power of the imagination.

There is no futuristic element in any of the fiction which Gloag published after the end of the second world war. *Tomorrow's Yesterday* was reprinted in 1946 in an omnibus along with ten short stories from *It Makes a Nice Change* and ten previously uncollected stories. One of the new stories, "Petrified," is science fiction, but it is merely a vignette dealing with an unfortunate side-effect of a drug whose effects are similar to that described in Wells's "The New Accelerator." Later, this notion was reversed in the contemporary thriller *Slow* (1954), in which an Englishman visiting France is caught up in a complicated web of intrigue as assorted spies compete to win control of a drug which slows down the metabolism. Gloag's last collection of short stories, *Take One a Week* (1950—an omnibus absorbing both the previous collections and adding new material), also has a couple of

21

borderline science fiction stories, but they are conventional stories of thought-transmission. By 1945, it seems, the creative impulse that had led him to write his major speculative works had been transformed, and from then on his energies were directed into other avenues. This is perhaps not surprising when one recalls that the advent of the atom bomb led to an outpouring of futuristic fantasies anxious about the possibility of a new war that might destroy civilization. There was no need for Gloag to participate; for him, it was all in the past. He had realized and dramatized the importance of the relevant trends fifteen years earlier, and to the man who had imagined radiant inflammatol in 1934 the atom bomb came as no particular surprise.

In 1946, with the war over, Gloag seems to have felt rather more cheerful than when he wrote *99%*. The preface which he wrote for *First One and Twenty*, the omnibus which included *Tomorrow's Yesterday*, defends the writing of stories for pure entertainment, and describes speculative fiction as an essentially playful endeavor. He quotes with approval a letter written to him by Olaf Stapledon, which says:

> All this modish playing about with time and space, which you and I have so often indulged in, is of course symptomatic of our period. It opens up new worlds for the writer of fantastic fiction, or at any rate gives him a new and exciting game to play. The rules of the game are imposed on him by the new attitude to time and space, but he can go beyond the accepted conditions as much as he likes, so long as he does not actually or flagrantly violate them, and so become implausible or even positively incredible.[13]

Gloag adds his own comment, to this effect:

> The writers of the popular scientific fantasy fiction have created a golden age of their own, projected into the not too distant future, where everything is streamlined, mechanised and appallingly tidy; where atomic energy has been safely harnessed, and life is organised by an aristocracy of technicians. This literature, with its own conventions and jargon, is a manifestation of the scientific romantic movement of which Jules Verne and H. G. Wells are the great progenitors. It responds to contemporary influences, and since the beginning of the second world war has seldom featured the catastrophic theme. This theme may not be so popular in the future when so many of us have had first hand experience of large scale catastrophe.[14]

Further on, he seems almost to be repenting of his own novels of ideas when he says that:

> Between the wars political, economic and sociological themes were tried and found wanting in entertainment value. Still, there may well be a healthy, creative reaction against the violence and solemnity of the last thirty years.[15]

Certainly, the fiction which Gloag produced in the years after the war is designed to entertain, and his novels of that period are not novels of ideas in the sense that his speculative novels certainly are. He defended the same point of view in 1950, and minimized the role played by ideas in his fiction, noting in one of his letters that,

> Your analysis of the characters in *Manna* suggests that you are reading far more into that tale than there is in it, if I may put it so very bluntly. I'm not conscious of trying to make my puppets convey anything in particular. Some wit, writing about H. G. Wells took some liberties with Holy Writ, and said that Wells "had sold his birthright for a spot of message," for he unashamedly wrote propaganda novels, which often seriously marred his great powers as a teller of tales. Apart from a desire to prod my readers and to bring them to the brink of "the dark river of thought" (another quotation from Wells, by the way), I was always intent on telling the story, as it had first come into my mind, and the sermon element was never considered at all. But remember, those semi-scientific romances written in the late thirties and early forties, were written when my life, and the lives of most people in this country, was shadowed by fear: the fear of war, air-raids, and (for a brief space) invasion.

It would, of course, be wrong to treat any of the novels described herein as propaganda, but it must be noted that Wells wrote various novels of ideas before he "sold his birthright for a spot of message," and the fact that his early scientific romances were written as popular thrillers does not in the least affect the fact that they contain some very serious (and sometimes deeply pessimistic) reflections on the place of men in nature and the future prospects of our civilization. Novels written to entertain may still be worth taking seriously as exemplifications of a particular view of the world, and the fact that a novel is entertaining should not mean—and very rarely does—that it is a mere literary confection, forgotten as soon as it is consumed.

It is always easy for a literary critic to confuse the intentional and the incidental, or at least to fail to discriminate well enough between different kinds of intention; but that which was unintended, or intended differently from the way it is interpreted, may nevertheless be interesting and revealing. I would not wish to mislead anyone into thinking that the novels of John Gloag are unduly ponderous by concentrating too hard on what they reveal about the outlook of the author. They are a joy to read, but they do indeed bring their readers to the brink of the dark river of thought, and compel them to look over it.

The work of John Gloag exemplifies both the deep gulf that lay between British and American speculative fiction between the wars, and the manner in which that breach was healed in the post-war period.

In America, the *genre* acquired a label, which created common cause simply by establishing a category-heading. Many of the American writers who made significant contributions to the *genre* between 1918 and 1945 wrote for the science fiction magazines, aware of other work that was appearing there. The fiction which these writers produced was predominantly optimistic about technological progress and confident about the future of American society. Future wars occur regularly in American science fiction of this period, but very few stories show any great anxiety about the possible effects of such wars. (It is significant that in the novel which features the bleakest scenes of devastation, L. Ron Hubbard's *Final Blackout*, it is

Europe that is destroyed—America recovers and consolidates her position as the most highly-developed nation on Earth.)

British speculative fiction of this period does not, of course, consist entirely of images of future devastation, but there is in virtually all of it an undercurrent of anxiety. The first world war left a far greater impact on the consciousness of Britons than on the Americans whose territory was never seriously threatened. The prospect of a second European war was far more frightful in the British imagination than in the American. The depression of the thirties had surprisingly little effect on the temper of American futuristic fiction (except, perhaps, to aid the proliferation of pulp science fiction by sustaining a heavy demand for escapist fantasies in a cheap format). Throughout the thirties, therefore, speculative fiction in America remained overwhelmingly committed to the myth of the inevitability of material progress, while British writers already felt that they had adequate reason to be suspicious of it. America inherited that suspicion after the second world war, and that is why it is possible to find a curious kinship between the images prevalent in British speculative fiction between the wars and American science fiction of the post-war decades.

The work of John Gloag testifies to this kinship by virtue of his ambivalent cynicism, his occasional sharp satire, and his anxious contemplation of the possibility of the catastrophic reversal of the pattern of social evolution. In view of this fact, it is curious that he has not attracted more attention from American scholars interested in the development of speculative fiction—perhaps because (as with so many British writers) his works were never widely available in the U.S. and could not call attention to themselves. They would repay such attention, for they are doubly revealing. They are, on the one hand, typical of a particular perception of the affairs of modern man that was generated by the historical circumstances of the period; and they are also the work of an ingenious and skillful writer—a genuine craftsman in prose—whose appeal has not been diminished by the dating of his visions of the future.

II.

ALGEBRAIC FANTASIES

THE SCIENCE FICTION OF BOB SHAW

The journal *Foundation* has a regular feature consisting of a series of auto-biographical essays by leading SF writers. More than twenty have appeared to date, under the general title of "The Profession of Science Fiction." The most fascinating aspect of the series is not the biographical information offered by the various con-tributors, much of which is already available (in skeletal form, at least) by courtesy of interviews conducted on behalf of the fan press; but rather the choices made by the authors as regards matters of emphasis. The essays are remarkably various in terms of what the authors find it necessary or desirable to say about themselves and their endeavors. Their strategies of self-analysis and self-justification are far more revealing than anything which is likely to emerge from an inteview whose structure and direction are controlled by the choices of others.

Bob Shaw's contribution to this series is an account of the metamorphosis of an "active and gregarious youngster" first into a science fiction fan and then into a writer. Presumably, most of the other contributors to the series must have under-gone a parallel transformation, but few of them discuss it in any detail, and several not at all. By comparison, Shaw's account is careful and painstaking, giving the impression that he has his own life-history under a microscope, subject to intensive and inquisitive scrutiny. That he should choose to approach the essay in this way is significant in two ways: it reveals the extent to which the special enthusiasm which Shaw enjoyed as a convert to the cause of science fiction still permeates his outlook, and hence his work; and it displays the ability to take a step back from everyday ex-periences to look at them with an inquiring, almost disinterested, eye. This capacity to detach himself from the familiar in order to bring it into a new focus is the talent that underlies his best work, whose hallmark is the seamless integration of imagina-tive inventions with events and actions which are archetypally *ordinary*.

Shaw explains in his *Foundation* article how the exotic aspects of science fiction met in him "the pressing need to escape from the suburban Belfast in the late 1930s":

> The discovery of *Astounding*, when I was about 11, converted me from a lover of science fiction into a rabid fanatic. The first thing I ever read in it was one of van Vogt's stories in the Mixed Men series, with its haughty Grand Captain Gloria Laurr and her vast warship from Imperial Earth hunting down a long-lost race of androids in the Magellanic Clouds. Looking back on the experi-ence, I could almost make a case for governmental control of the exposure of vintage van Vogt to developing minds. The effect on me was much more devastating than LSD and much longer last-

ing—indeed, as far as I can determine, it was indelible. The boys'
paper science fiction had been intriguing, but not wholly satisfying, whereas in the van Vogt stories there was a soul-glutting
blend of new concepts, politics, sex, and adventure. His palette
was sombre-hued, the brush strokes were broad, and the overall
impression was one of sophisticated brooding maturity which I
found totally irresistible.

It is no exaggeration to say that the reading of that first story
changed the entire course of my life.[1]

He goes on to substantiate the claim that this encounter with van Vogt
changed his life by explaining how reading SF distracted him in the classroom,
and—later—how as an apprentice draughtsman he blighted his chances of advancement by quitting night school in order to have sufficient time to work on fanzines.
He comments that "I was utterly without worldly ambition because I *knew* that all
that was needed for a rich full life was a few shillings a week with which to buy SF
magazines and beer."

The picture which Shaw paints of parental misunderstanding and disap-
proval is a bleak one; the way of life and thought into which he was encouraged by
his involvement with SF contrasted sharply with the expectations and values generated by the dour culture of the Protestant Ethic in one of its narrower manifestations. No matter how complete a metamorphosis a man may achieve, his past still
clings to him, and the tension between the world-view which Shaw inherited and the
one he discovered was inevitably maintained in his feelings:

One side of my nature was fervently convinced that devotion
to science fiction was the path to happiness; the other side was
keenly aware of my father's disappointment and shared his conviction that a life of industrious respectability in a recognised safe
job was no more than the family's due.[2]

This ambivalence is clearly something that still affects Shaw's outlook, and
it is visible in much of his fiction, where his heroes very frequently find themselves
caught between the irreconcilable demands of domesticity and ambition. One of the
most striking features of Shaw's work is the way in which the domestic environment
(which plays a more crucial role in his fiction than is typical of *genre* SF) is almost
always portrayed as bleak, overdemanding, and hurtful.

It is not surprising, in the light of Shaw's representation of his conversion,
that the extended piece of fan fiction, "The Enchanted Duplicator," planned by
Shaw in the early fifties (though mostly written by Walt Willis) takes the form that
it does. It is a parody of *The Pilgrim's Progress*, detailing Jophan's journey from
the land of Mundane to the world of Trufandom, beset by many perils. Much is
made of the necessity of maintaining a sense of humor, represented in the story as a
shield. The shield is used in the novelette mainly to ward off the rocks hurled by
abrasive fanzine reviewers, but its defensive capabilities are obviously much
greater, as Jophan is careful never to relax his grip upon it. Shaw remains one of
the great humorists of the fan community—his comic essays, usually first revealed
as "serious scientific talks" at conventions, have won him two Hugos for "Best Fan
Writer"—and he possesses a distinctive, rather self-effacing, style. When giving his
talks he seems ill-at-ease; he speaks slowly, in a deadpan manner, usually waiting
for the endorsement of audience laughter before acknowledging his own jokes. The
impression remains that a "Shield of Umor" has provided Bob Shaw with vital pro-

tective cover throughout his life in Mundane. For a long time, it seems, he was only able to take science fiction seriously by pretending that it was a "bit of a joke."

The same tension between the dullness of mundanity and the excitement of imaginative extravagance is evident in Shaw's personal manifesto for science fiction as an art-form, which he defends eloquently in the *Foundation* essay. It is perhaps revealing that he passes from discussion of his early experiences in life to a rather abstract polemic in defence of SF without so much as a textual break:

> So much for early influences. Currently, I regard science fiction as escapist, but in a positive sense. The conventional way of taking time off from the pressures of existence is to narrow one's field, to retreat inwards to the miniature and more controllable world of the model railway, the garden, the budgerigar in its cage. Equivalents in literature are the western and the mystery novel—especially the country house whodunnit—in which the boundaries of the observed universe are drawn in tight, like chintz curtains, and the actions are performed by a cast of simplified characters.
>
> Science fiction escapism is different because it is an escape *to* reality.
>
> The world image presented by mundane "realists" is one in which the invariants are things like mortgages, the TUC, engine wear, national insurance contributions, prostate troubles, Sunday, unemployment figures, newspapers, cemeteries, Harpic, ambition, season tickets, raincoats, Russia, suet, gas meters, greenfly, and so on. What the science fiction buff understands is that all these things are merely local phenomena of a very temporary nature, and that to get them in their proper perspective it is only necessary to step back a few thousand light years. That is where the excitement lay in my discovery of science fiction—and what a relief to learn that its verities so greatly transcended the paltry reality which so much engaged the attention of others.
>
> It's all a matter of viewpoint, of course. A person who is reading the minutes of a trade union conference probably feels that he is in closer contact with reality than another who is reading—to choose a very basic example—a story about a spaceship getting into difficulties and being forced to land on an unfamiliar world. And yet he is concerning himself with a transient local phenomenon, while the SF reader is projecting himself into a general class of situation which must have occurred many times in countless galaxies throughout the universe. To put it another way: reportage is arithmetic; fiction is algebra.[3]

This is, of course, a neat and clever inversion of a common argument. From the point of view of the world in which Shaw grew up, science fiction is pure fantasy—arbitrary, irrational, and experientially worthless. Everything which lies beyond the horizons of the commonplace is considered to be devoid of meaning. Shaw is not content simply to deny this; instead he turns the argument around and redirects the accusation without reducing its force. Thus, the world of the imagination becomes the standard, and passes judgment upon the meaning and significance of everyday experience. The preoccupation with the mundane and the oppressive-.

ness of circumstance becomes aberrant: arbitrary in its shortsightedness, irrational in its evaluations, and experientially worthless.

Bob Shaw is not a didactic writer in the usual sense of the term: he does not preach any political creed or moral doctrine. He is a storyteller and an entertainer. Nevertheless, his work partakes of a certain crusading zeal. He is a careful writer, aware of what he is doing and what has to be done. He is an ambassador from a greater world, who intends to show us the narrowness of the "reality" which threatens us from the other side. For him, science fiction—*because* it is exciting and entertaining and escapist—can introduce its readers to a better way of being. To extend his own metaphor, he wants to lure his readers away from the dull transactions of known quantities, whose sums and multiplications invariably point to fixed and familiar answers, to the world of *unknown* quantities where x and y stand for infinite possibilities, and the solution to every equation is masked, ready to surprise us when we have worked through the logic of our calculation.

After several years of dedicated fan activity, during which time he made his professional debut in an American newspaper, Shaw began to place stories with the minor professional SF magazines which co-existed with *New Worlds* in the UK. In 1954-56 he published five stories in *Nebula* and one in *Authentic*. The first of them, "Aspect," tells of a group of space-explorers who discover a curious artifact on a barren world. This turns out to be one room in a house whose doors are matter-transmitters and whose parts are scattered about several worlds. They find that this particular room has been placed specifically to provide a lovely view of the sunrise over a mountain peak—a peak which they must destroy in order to take off. In a sequel, "Sounds in the Dawn," the builders of the strange house trap the fleeing explorers and subject them to a trial by ordeal. Like the other stories of this period, these early efforts are amateurish—clumsy embodiments of ideas which carry a spark of originality without being of much interest.

Shaw has said that on rereading these stories once he could detach himself sufficiently to weigh them accurately he found them so conspicuously wanting that he decided to sideline his ambitions as a writer until he felt competent to do himself justice, and for nearly a decade he made hardly any attempt to publish professionally. He had one more story in *Nebula*—"The Silent Partners" in 1959—of which he thought well enough to include it in one of his collections; a collaboration with Walt Willis appeared in *If* the following year, but he did not resume his assault upon the professional markets with any commitment until 1965.

The decision to give up writing was in some ways a curious one. A great many writers, no doubt, look back on their earliest published material with embarrassment, and there can be very few who find that their effort has matched their intentions. Most, however, keep on going in pursuit of the well-established principle that practice makes perfect. Shaw seems to have felt that what was lacking in his work was not so much literary skill and craftsmanship as the raw material on which he might draw. I have heard him say that he felt the need of more experience of the world; and though it may seem paradoxical that a writer who believes that SF is essentially escapist should want to gather more experience of the mundane world before considering himself competent to write it, there is no contradiction involved. Shaw has always been concerned with the difficult problem of constructing a *lived-in world* for his characters rather than a mere stage on which the products of his imagination may parade—the connection and tension between the extraordinary and the mundane is, as I have already pointed out, his hallmark.

During the years that Shaw was preparing himself for new ventures in fiction he worked for a while in Canada and followed several professions. From his work in draughtsmanship and structural engineering he moved into industrial public relations and then into journalism. In the meantime, he fostered the education which he had once been prepared to neglect; like many science fiction writers, he eventually cultivated a body of knowledge *and* wisdom rather more widespread (if also more idiosyncratic) than the prepackaged product marketed in schools. By means of eccentric self-education he acquired an invaluable sensitivity to unusual items of information, and the ability to throw information into new perspective by adopting an unfamiliar point of view.

His career as a writer was launched again in Michael Moorcock's *New Worlds*, where he seemed a hardened traditionalist among the experimenters of the "new wave." "...And Isles Where Good Men Lie" and "Pilot Plant" are both fast-moving stories—the second so crowded with incident that it seems almost to be a drastically-abridged novel. In the former story the hero is the one man who figures out how to stop a bizarre invasion of Earth; in the latter the hero is freed by a freak accident from a compulsion earlier placed upon him by aliens stranded in orbit and needing spare parts for their starship. In both stories the central character is beset by personal problems which provide an extra dimension of threat to his chances of solving his problems. In these early stories the solution of the technical problems is supplemented (albeit rather haphazardly) by the resolution of the personal problems, but in later work Shaw has tended to reject such sleight-of-hand. Characteristically, his heroes find it easier to save the world than to save themselves.

The next story which Shaw published—this time in *Analog*—posted an unmistakeable signpost to his future success, and has become established as one of the classic stories of its period. This was "Light of Other Days," the story which introduced the notion of slow glass. It was a Nebula nominee, and had it been the work of a writer whose name was already familiar it would surely have won (it was, in fact, beaten by Richard McKenna's posthumously-published, "The Secret Place"). "Light of Other Days" is a highly distinctive story in which an idea with all kinds of marvellous potentialities is elegantly revealed by a subtle inversion of perspective in a domestic context. In the story, windows made of a glass which drastically retards light are bought by town-dwellers from "farms" established in regions of scenic beauty, so that they may look out of their living rooms and see—for a time—a more beautiful world than their immediate environs. (The similarity between this notion and that of the alien house in "Aspect" is interesting, and it is easy to see the emotional appeal of the idea in the context of Shaw's autobiographical essay.) The narrator, touring with his family in the country, approaches a glass-farmer in the hope of buying a window more cheaply than by patronizing a city department store. He completes his transaction successfully, but is puzzled by the behavior of the farmer in respect of the windows of his own house, through which a woman and child can occasionally be glimpsed. In the quiet climax of the story this suddenly begins to make sense—the final insight depends on a semi-obvious property of the glass, but refers not to any technological miracle, concentrating instead on the psychological utility of the substance. The way in which the narrator's relationship with his family is economically developed, and neatly juxtaposed with the farmer's relationship with *his*, is quite brilliant.

In a sequel to "Light of Other Days" published the following year, "Burden of Proof," Shaw deals with equal delicacy with the emotions of a judge awaiting the emergence from a pane of slow glass of the image of a murder committed several years previously, which will either confirm or deny the propriety of his judgment in sentencing a man to death. These stories could not begin to exhaust the imaginative consequences of the premise, however, and Shaw was later to take up the challenge ·

of explicating the total effect of the hypothetical discovery of slow glass upon human society in the novel *Other Days, Other Eyes*.

Along with "Pilot Plant" and "Light of Other Days," Shaw published one more story in 1966: "Call Me Dumbo." It is exceptional within his canon both in featuring a female protagonist and for the cold-blooded brutality of its ironic climax. The story is the record of the protagonist's slow awakening to intelligent self-consciousness. Previously she has been kept in a drugged state by her "husband," but her supply of the drug has been accidentally denatured by one of her children. She has been living a dull and humdrum domestic existence quietly and without question, but as intelligence and curiosity return she realizes that things are not as they seem. She finds, in fact, that her cosy home is the sole human habitation on an alien world, where a spaceship has crashed leaving only two survivors. The whole truth about herself and her husband, when she learns it, is horrific—but her reaction has to take into account the force of necessity which led her companion to take the cruel course of action which he did. She can take a kind of revenge on him, but the only fate she can make for herself is even more cruel in its way, involving a voluntary retreat back into drugged stupor, where all she can perceive is the drab, false mundanity which has contained her for so long. Only an ardent believer in escapism—escapism *to* reality—could demonstrate so powerfully the awfulness of a situation where such an escape is untenable; "Call Me Dumbo" is the bleakest story Shaw has ever written.

Shaw's first novel, *Night Walk*, was published in 1967. It is a fast-moving suspense story in which a secret agent from Earth is trapped on the world of Emm Luther with vital information literally locked away in his brain.

In the universe of the story travel between the stars has been made possible by hyperspatial "corridors" linked by "portals." Null-space thus allows access to the whole universe, but is impossible to navigate except by means of complex routes through long series of portals. For this reason, only a handful of habitable planets are accessible to the expanding human population, and the discovery of a new one (whose location is the secret in Sam Tallon's brain) promises to precipitate a territorial war between Earth and its main colony, Emm Luther.

In the opening chapters of the narrative Tallon is captured by the sadistic Cherkassky, who sets out to destroy his mind. Tallon makes a temporary getaway, severely injuring his tormentor in the process, but in retaliation Cherkassky blinds him. Once in prison, though, the warden Helen Juste exploits his engineering skills by allowing him to work in collaboration with other prisoners to develop a device transmitting images recorded by other eyes into his own brain. Her motive is to free her brother from his own blindness, and she confiscates one of two sets that Tallon and his collaborators construct; but with the aid of the other set Tallon and a second blind man succeed in escaping. His companion is killed but Tallon, against all odds, manages to stay alive in the hostile world. After a second, and highly melodramatic, confrontation with Cherkassky, Tallon escapes from Emm Luther and is enabled by his device for borrowing the sight of other eyes to make a discovery which dramatically transforms the oppressive situation that is driving the human race into a bitter war.

In *Night Walk* Shaw makes no attempt to cultivate a naturalistic mode of presentation. The wheels of the plot are turned by the gears of outrageous coincidence and melodramatic flourishes are very much the order of the day. It stands out among Shaw's novels in featuring a hero who conforms to a particular *genre*-fiction stereotype—the man alone, whose performance within the plot is entirely self-contained. All of Shaw's other heroes are entangled and constrained, at least to some extent, in domestic relationships which control and counterbalance their involvement with extraordinary events. The mundane world features in *Night Walk* only as a curiously out-of-place landscape: the vast suburbia which apparently covers virtually all the land surface of Emm Luther and which (as the planet's name suggests) is supposedly ruled by a newly puritanical Protestant Ethic.

Night Walk was originally published under the new imprint of Banner Books, and enjoyed remarkably poor distribution until later reprinted by Avon, Banner's parent company. Shaw's next novel, *The Two-Timers*, had the benefit of a much better release, appearing in the U.S. as one of the Ace Science Fiction Specials edited by Terry Carr, and in Britain from Victor Gollancz. It is a better novel, less frenetic in its pace and less melodramatic than its predecessor, and is much more typical of his work as a whole. It develops a dramatic contrast between the tensions of everyday existence and the imaginative consequences of a science-fictional premise.

The novel begins when the world of John Breton, an engineer becalmed in an embittered and uncomfortable marriage, is invaded by an *alter ego* who has come to claim his wife. Nine years earlier, Breton had caused his wife to walk alone across the city at night in the wake of a petty quarrel. In the world of his *alter ego* Jack, Kate Breton was murdered; the event transformed Jack's life and diverted his energies into the obsessive development of a time machine which would allow him to save her. In John's world Kate *was* saved, by a mysterious person resembling him closely, who appeared at the crucial moment and shot the would-be murderer. John Breton has been enjoying the consequences of this "miracle" for nine years, allowing his life to develop along the path already foreshadowed in the fatal quarrel. His marriage is now apparently close to the borders of intolerability—but the "solution" offered by Jack's arrival does not strike him as an appropriate one, and causes him to review his situation and personal history from a new perspective.

Two further factors complicate the plot of the novel: the presence of a detective who has always believed, in spite of the apparent impossibility, that it was John Breton who shot his wife's attacker; and the "side-effects" of Jack Breton's transfer from one universe to another, disturbing the symmetrical distribution of mass between the two. Though the latter set of complications eventually threatens to escalate to apocalyptic dimensions, and compels the story to reach its climax in due time, the real focus of interest in the novel is the unprecedented interplay of character between the three leading figures. The conclusion of the story restores the balance of circumstances, but it is all the more effective because of what it leaves *unsettled*: the vital question of how the protagonists will learn how to live with themselves now that they know how things might have been. There is a crucial gap between what can be achieved by the author's weaving of the threads of the plot and what is left untouched by such manipulation.

Similar contrasts are a regular feature of the novels of what might be called Shaw's first prolific period (1965-72), where the science-fictional problems which are presumed to confront the whole human race are generally resolved, while the personal problems enveloping the central characters are generally shown to be (in equivalent terms) insoluble—they will yield only to extreme compromise and self-sacrifice. Curiously, this pattern is something which is largely absent from the novels of his second prolific period (1976-79), appearing only in *A Wreath of Stars*. The reason for this may be that Shaw is a writer who has always tried to resist the temptation to be formularistic in his approach, and may have begun avoiding the pattern as soon as he became aware that it *was* a pattern. It would be ironic if it were so, for this element of contrast is aesthetically powerful in virtually all of the novels where it occurs, and serves to make some of the early novels more satisfying and more memorable than some of the later ones, in spite of the fact that the later ones show significant improvements in other aspects of writing technique.

In 1969 Shaw published two novels. One of them, *Shadow of Heaven*, is the weakest of all his longer works. The plot moves jerkily, and it lacks both the fast pace of *Night Walk* and the theatrical complexity of *The Two-Timers* (it was actually written before these earlier-published works). Its hero travels from the overcrowded urban wilderness of America's eastern seaboard to the floating pasturelands suspended by antigravity devices high in the sky. There he plays a role in the breaking of the political machine which exploits the produce and the mystique of the platform and others like it. The aesthetic appeal of the basic premise is considerable, but it makes little logical sense; the premises required to support the basic image clearly have different consequences if properly extended. Shaw is actually too careful and conscientious a writer to conceal his own realization of these logical flaws from the reader, and they become obvious in the story as his attempts to paper over the cracks become increasingly awkward. The thinking which Shaw was forced to do about the working of limited anti-gravity devices was not, however, wasted.

The other novel published in the same year, *The Palace of Eternity*, is very different. Its hero, Mack Tavernor, has retreated from involvement in a galaxy-wide interracial war to a strange world named Mnemosyne, whose sky is littered with the debris of two shattered moons. It is a world beloved by artists, among whom Tavernor feels himself to be something of an alien, but as the story opens it is being invaded by military forces, because Earth's high command has decided for mysterious reasons to transfer its headquarters there. Though Tavernor has held the rank of Colonel, and was the inventor of a weapon which is crucial to the success of humans involved in close combat with the alien enemy, he finds himself just as antagonistic to the military as the artists. One man in particular—Gervaise Farrell—poses a direct threat to him in becoming the most likely candidate for the hand of the girl he loves. When the antagonism between the artists and the soldiers flares up into violence, Tavernor becomes an outlaw—a decision which ultimately costs him everything, including his life.

The first part of the novel, which deals with Tavernor's decisions and actions in a situation which is painful to start with and which grows steadily more desperate, is relentlessly sustained. It is a highly effective piece of writing, and though the entire story is set in alien surroundings, Shaw manages to make the account thoroughly convincing, mainly because of the effort he devotes to making Tavernor's thoughts and feelings believable in the context of his personal history. The novel then undergoes a complete change of nature. Some readers have complained that the metamorphosis is too much to cope with, and that the novel disintegrates thereafter; others, by contrast, have found the final section quite awe-inspiring. As in all three novels so far considered, Shaw places the whole human race in an existential predicament which is inexorably getting worse. Here, as in *The Two-Timers*, the threat is apocalyptic, but it is by no means a threat which can be countered so simply; no human action within the situation as designed can be adequate—in order for there to be salvation it is necessary that the existential context should be completely transformed and the parameters of human capability transcended.

This kind of transcendental transformation of desperate situations is, of course, the main stock-in-trade of the writer whose *Astounding* novelette had such a powerful effect on the young Bob Shaw: A. E. van Vogt. It is a device which van Vogt overuses, and which he employs in an entirely arbitrary fashion, but which nevertheless retains the power to impart a dramatic shock to the reader who encounters it unsuspectingly for the first time. In *The Palace of Eternity* Shaw attempts to pull off his own *coup* of this kind. However, though Shaw was later to pay homage to van Vogt in another work (the fix-up novel *Ship of Strangers*), he is by no means a van Vogtian writer in the sense that, for example, Charles Harness or Ian Wallace might be so described. Shaw delights in surprising his readers, but he has never gone in for arbitrary plot-twists, nor for deliberate obscurantism by means of "intensive recomplication." He is imaginatively economical *within* his works, despite the fact that when taken as a whole they show considerable ideative fertility. For these reasons, the greater context into which Shaw switches his plot following the death of its central character is not at all similar to the kind of context van Vogt usually uses; and in particular, its central motif of burgeoning superhumanity is handled *very* differently.

Tavernor, after his death, learns a terrible truth about the nature of man and the unwitting consequences of man's conquest of space. Shaw invokes a science-fictional explanation of the survival of the *persona* after death, but introduces a second premise which puts this secular salvation under threat. In order to secure the salvation which humans, unknowingly, already are heir to, Tavernor must be reborn as his own son, to be raised in an atmosphere of intemperate hatred by the man who married his lover, Gervaise Farrell. From this desperate situation, eventually brought to a climax by the invasion of Mnemosyne by the alien enemy, Tavernor must redeem himself in order to secure the future of his species: a future very different from any that could have been envisaged from the viewpoint of his first existence.

The Palace of Eternity is a novel intended to take its readers (in its own words) "beyond Man's wildest imaginings." This is, of course, a paradoxical prospectus, and there is a sense in which all novels of this kind must fail. All that can really be done is to post a signpost pointing from the realms of the imaginable to the hinterlands of possibility that lie beyond their horizons. The impressiveness of such endeavors depends not so much on how well the transformation of perspective is accomplished, nor on the competence with which the new state of being is suggestively represented, but on the extent to which the reader has been convinced by the naturalistic part of the story that such a transcendence is *necessary*. (As all evangelists know, people are made ready for promises of salvation by first being convinced of the threat of damnation.) The effectiveness of the final part of *The Palace of Eternity* is really dependent on the extent to which the first part succeeds in representing the hopelessness of the hero's (and the human race's) situation. In this respect, it has to contend with the expectations of the habitual *genre* reader, who is used to omnicompetent heroes who will get the girl and vanquish the enemy no matter how heavy the odds. It is a tribute to Shaw's ability that, at least for a good many readers, he succeeded.

No novel of the species to which *The Palace of Eternity* belongs can ever really live up to its own ambitions, and the most which can be said even for the best such novels is that they will stick in the memory as worthy efforts to make an important but elusive point. It will probably be the case that *The Palace of Eternity*, like Clifford D. Simak's *Time and Again* and Arthur C. Clarke's *Childhood's End*, will grow in reputation as it ages, though its contribution to the mythology of SF may be considered less because it is anticipated to some extent by both these earlier novels.

After such a conceptually extravagant novel as *The Palace of Eternity* a writer is inevitably faced with the problem of what to do next that will not seem pale by comparison, and it is by no means surprising that Shaw elected for a complete change of pace. His next novel, *One Million Tomorrows*, is sparing in its use of imagination, belonging to the sub-*genre* of SF in which an author attempts to track the impact on social and personal life of a single hypothetical innovation. In this case, the innovation is a drug permitting extreme longevity which has the unfortunate side-effect of rendering men impotent.

This kind of story presents a considerable challenge to the ingenuity and discipline of a writer, and there are remarkably few attempts which actually succeed in turning the trick. Very few SF writers actually attempt it; it requires both intellectual subtlety and a capacity for narrative realism, which are rare enough individually, let alone in combination. Shaw undoubtedly has both, though it is dubious whether he was able to marshal these resources at the stage of his career when he set out to write *One Million Tomorrows*, which is less than half-successful.

The effect that potential immortality might have on its recipients is a matter well-considered by SF writers, though their thoughts tend to run along stereotyped channels. This, however, is a subject which Shaw barely touches; his interest is concentrated instead on the adjustments of sexual morality and personal relationships which follow on from the supposition that males, at some stage in their life, have to sacrifice potency in favor of defeating the aging process. The focal point for the examination of these adjustments is the marriage of the story's protagonist, Will Carewe. Shaw is reluctant, though, to let the domestic tensions carry the weight of the story, and submerges this aspect of the novel beneath a melodramatic "hide-and-seek" plot in which the hero flees to Africa and back while trying to dodge would-be assassins and trying to figure out who has it in for him and why. For this reason, *One Million Tomorrows* falls uncomfortably between stools. As a novel of ideas it lacks depth and penetration, while as a mystery-and-mayhem adventure story it is somewhat half-hearted. Shaw must have realized this, for in the two novels which followed *One Million Tomorrows*—both of which elaborate the consequences of single innovations in a near-contemporary context—he made far more strenuous and effective attempts to achieve dramatic coherence (despite, in the latter case, the fact that the narrative is highly episodic). These two novels were *Ground Zero Man* and *Other Days, Other Eyes*.

Ground Zero Man is based on a hypothesis which is far from uncommon in imaginative fiction: it is the story of a relatively insignificant man who stumbles upon a discovery which gives him the power to bring about a drastic alteration in the world's balance of military power (in this case, he can detonate the world's stockpiles of nuclear weapons by remote control.) Thus cast into a moral dilemma for which he is entirely unprepared, he must accept the uncalled-for responsibility of making a decision that might affect the future of mankind.

It is almost traditional that in stories of this kind the lone scientist should set out to put the world to rights, if necessary by blackmail. Shaw's Lucas Hutchman is no exception. When stories like this were written in the nineteenth century—examples include Ignatius Donnelly's *The Golden Bottle* (1892) and Simon Newcomb's *His Wisdom the Defender* (1900)—the heroes tended to be successful in imposing their benevolent will, but twentieth-century writers have grown steadily more pessimistic about the prospect facing isolated individuals attempting to combat the insanity of the masses. The novel with which *Ground Zero Man* has most in common is C. S. Forester's bitter novel, *The Peacemaker* (1934), whose hero is motivated to take his stand partly as a result of his disastrous marital situation, and who ultimately finds the world so intractable that he is literally torn to pieces by the mob. Shaw's Hutchman is exaggerated in his social isolation by the neurotic jealousy of his wife, and this plays no small part in determining the shape of his plan to save the world. And, like Forester's peacemaker, he seems to be taking on far more than he can possibly handle, for all that he seems to be a wiser man.

Like Will Carewe, Hutchman is rapidly driven into a deadly game of hide-and-seek, but here the dramatic tension arises quite naturally from the initial hypothesis. The uneasy coincidences of *Night Walk's* big chase are nowhere in evidence, and the split-second timing of the climax seems quite appropriate in context. The eventual resolution revealed by the epilogue fits perfectly without being predictable. Though it is not so striking in its ideative originality as Shaw's other novels of the period, it is a satisfying and successful work; paradoxically, though, it enjoyed little success—it did not appear in Britain until 1976, and then only in a paperback edition.

In *Other Days, Other Eyes* Shaw undertook a notoriously difficult—but also notoriously lucrative—exercise: the building of a full-length novel around a highly-successful short story. At the time of its writing, Shaw was known first and foremost as "the man who invented slow glass," and he had an excellent opportunity to make something more of a fascinating notion whose possibilities extended far beyond the scope of the original story and its sequel. The extent to which society might be transformed by such an invention was, as Shaw cleverly realized, much greater than was immediately evident.

Other Days, Other Eyes incorporates three short stories, including "Light of Other Days" and "Burden of Proof," which are labelled "sidelights," and which serve the purpose of extending the reader's perception of the implications of slow glass; but the novel is basically the story of Alban Garrod, the inventor whose career takes a dramatic turn when the light-retardation effect crops up unexpectedly while he is trying to engineer a specially-tough glass. The property first reveals itself as the discovered cause of several fatal accidents, and the story is preoccupied by the more baleful implications of the new product. Throughout the story it seems that scenic windows, no matter how popular they may be, are little enough compensation for the plague of troubles released from this innocent-seeming Pandora's Box. Garrod becomes rich, but even that has its sour side as the dramatic change in the economic balance of power within his marriage embitters his relationship with his wife. As the effects of slow glass insidiously extend through the social world, so they continue to be seen at a more immediate level in Garrod's own life. The crucial experiment which allows technical control of the information-release from slow glass also serves, through a tragic accident, to destroy his wife's sight. Like Sam Tallon, Garrod builds a device that will allow her to borrow the sight of other eyes, but the other eyes which she requisitions are his own—a fact which threatens to bind him to her forever, although there is a chance of his finding happiness if he can escape from her grip.

It cannot be said that *Other Days, Other Eyes* achieves the same classic status as a novel that "Light of Other Days" has as a short story. It is too preoccupied with the elegantly-plotted but ultimately trivial exercises in deduction by which Garrod thwarts the plans of ingenious criminals; these are effective enough in their own way, but give the impression of deflecting attention from the main issues. Nevertheless, the importance of the work should not be underestimated; it is one of a bare handful of science fiction novels which convincingly demonstrates the power that technology has for transforming social relations. It is easy enough for us to appreciate that the invention of a matter-transmitter or the harnessing of nuclear fusion might ultimately change the world out of all recognition, but a species of glass which simply slows down the velocity of light—which differs only in degree from the glass which we already have—is a much more modest invention. Shaw's careful and convincing demonstration of the fact that our world would be profoundly and fundamentally affected is highly effective in reminding us how precariously our way of life is balanced upon the fulcrum of possibility. It is, like all good science fiction, a fantasy with intellectual consequences, and its moral is well worth taking seriously.

From 1967 on, the bulk of Shaw's effort was devoted to his novels. In 1967-69 he published only four short stories, and with the exception of "Burden of Proof" all were trivial. "Hue and Cry" and "Element of Chance," indeed, are twist-in-the-tail stories that might equally well have been written for *Nebula* fifteen years previously. From 1970-72, however, Shaw's production of shorter works (or, at least, his ability to sell them) increased considerably. He appeared in virtually every major SF magazine, and though many of the stories were vignettes with no pretensions to seriousness, he was able to justify the publication of his first collection, *Tomorrow Lies in Ambush*, in 1973. The collection is not impressive, but does represent in part the lighter side of Shaw's imagination: frivolous, irreverent, and often delicate in its use of irony.

In "Repeat Performance" (1971) actors begin to step down from the screen in a small town movie-house, and the owner's attempt to tackle the problem with strict experimental rigor goes nicely awry. In "What Time d'You Call This?" (1971) a petty criminal borrows a mad scientist's device for hopping into parallel worlds, with embarrassing consequences. In "Communication" (1970) a computer salesman tries to let himself into a lucrative racket run by a fake spiritualist, with unexpected results. "The Weapons of Isher II" (1971) records some of the difficulties entailed in building guns purely for self-defense.

These are the kind of stories which Robert Sheckley and Robert Silverberg used to turn out with such fluid ease in the fifties (were it not for the existence of a famous namesake, one might observe an interesting coincidence of initials here). And, like these other writers, Shaw was able to get extra bite out of stories in which the jokes turn distinctly sour: "Telemart Three" (1970), for instance, is a projection of runaway consumerism whose final trick is as nasty as it is ingenious, and "Invasion of Privacy" (1970) is a decidedly unfunny horror story. A more complex, light-hearted story is "The Cosmic Cocktail Party" (1970), in which the minds of dead men are maintained in a computer so that they may continue to offer advice to the living, but which find other opportunities and other incentives available in their new circumstances.

The year when this first collection appeared marked a hiatus in Shaw's publications. The effect of holding down a daytime job and writing in the evenings was beginning to tell on him, as was the strain of bringing up his family in the troubled city of Belfast. He moved to England in 1973, but it was not until the middle of 1974 that his work again began appearing regularly, commencing with the serialization in *Galaxy* of *Orbitsville*.

Orbitsville is basically a space opera involving the discovery and the beginning of exploitation of a gigantic object enclosing a star. Like the secret of navigating null-space in *Night Walk*, the discovery is of tremendous significance owing to an urgent shortage of *lebensraum* in the universe where the story is situated. The discovery is made by Vance Garamond, who has been forced to flee the wrath of Elizabeth Lindstrom, the repulsive and psychotic ruler of Earth's commercial interplanetary empire. The discovery wins him freedom from immediate assassination, but Elizabeth Lindstrom blames him (unjustly) for the death of her son, and she remains determined to enjoy a suitable revenge. First she attempts to remove Garamond by means of a staged accident, but instead succeeds in stranding him inside Orbitsville, facing a homeward trek of some 15,000,000 kilometres. Garamond must face this all-but-impossible journey in order to save the life of his own son, the time of whose execution has been secretly set by his adversary.

Inevitably, *Orbitsville* is constantly compared to Larry Niven's *Ringworld* (a much smaller artifact!). Both novels deal with large-scale hardware left behind by mysterious technologists who have long since disappeared, leaving the inhabitants of their vast territories to decline into unambitious decadence. Niven, with a larger fan following and four years head start, did far better with *Ringworld*, in terms of awards and sales, than Shaw has done with *Orbitsville*—thus proving, if anyone was in doubt, that good tactics consist of getting there firstest with the mostest men—but there are several reasons for preferring the latter novel. It has greater dramatic tension throughout—Garamond's personal war with Elizabeth Lindstrom is of more immediate interest than the interplay between Niven's human and alien characters—and is perhaps marginally more effective in giving the reader some sense of the awful *immensity* of the artifact; but its real advantage lies in the way that the author steps back from the action of the story in the brief coda to show the reader, in a moment of revelation all the more startling for being deliberately understated, what Orbitsville's actual *significance* is for the immigrants who will live there.

Both novels contain as a central mystery the problem of *why* their giant artifacts were constructed, but Shaw is the writer who offers an answer so singularly appropriate as to compel acceptance. (Niven's eventual answer to the same question, given in *Ringworld Engineers*, seems banal and contrived by comparison.) The coda is only a single page of print, but it has the effect of transforming the reader's perspective. The imaginative consequences of its inclusion are quite stunning: we never do find out who built Orbitsville, but the mere fact of its existence allows us, thanks to the insight of the author, to deduce its purpose, and also justifies a conclusive and comprehensive reassessment of human destiny. That insight sets Shaw apart not only from Larry Niven but from a whole tradition in American science fiction; some readers might think it a pessimistic insight (and would probably think the same of the epilogue to *Ground Zero Man*), but it is misleading to see it in such a light; it is the calm, emotionally uncolored statement of a theorem which, though far from obvious, is actually entailed by the premises of the story.

Another, less important, feature of *Orbitsville* which is likely to draw the attention of the reader—and, indeed, likely to alienate some readers—is the remarkably uncharitable characterization of its leading female characters. Elizabeth Lindstrom is ugly and malicious, Garamond's wife is stupid and ineffectual. The climactic moment of the plot emphasizes all of this in a single striking picture of utter frustration. Indeed, on the basis of all Shaw's novels prior to *Orbitsville*, it would be very difficult to defend him from a charge of misogyny. The women in his stories are almost never represented sympathetically—especially the wives, each of whom is a millstone around the hero's neck, strangling him by means of jealousy, malice, or awkward helplessness. As previously noted, these desperate personal conflicts rarely reach any kind of resolution—capitulation with unpleasant inevitability is more common than conventional romantic success. This tendency became far less marked in the novels of the later prolific period, but it fades out only gradually.

The significance of this pattern, which is entirely atypical of science fiction, is hard to judge, but an important factor in explanation is undoubtedly the fact that it *is* so atypical. Shaw was, at least to some extent, attempting to break the pulp-fiction mold which cast most science-fictional heroes as free agents who would probably achieve romantic success (if they could be bothered) while in the process of saving mankind from dread perils. That kind of convention is antipathetic to

ALGEBRAIC FANTASIES & REALISTIC ROMANCES, by Brian Stableford

Shaw's *modus operandi* for two reasons: first, because of the way he derives dramatic tension from the juxtaposition and conflict between the lived-in world of domestic life and his extravagant science-fictional hypotheses; second, because (in consequence of this first point) he attempts more fully to characterize his heroes than many SF writers, and the description of a complex domestic situation is a valuable asset in processes of characterization. (It is always easier to demonstrate tension and conflict in relationships than harmony, and stories thrive on conflict.) Rather than this aspect of Shaw's work being a calculated insult to the female of the species, it is actually a purposive strategy on which he has grown slowly less dependent as he has become more confident in his command of narrative realism.

Orbitsville, though published after something of a gap in Shaw's production, nevertheless seems to invite consideration as the final work in the first phase of his career rather than the first work in the second phase. It was about the time of its book publication that he became a full-time writer, accepting the pressure of *having* to write constantly and consistently and *having* to sell his work. He planned on publishing two books a year from 1976 onward, and obtained a contract from his principal publisher which committed him to this rate of production. There seems little doubt that this decision affected the work which he then began to do, and there is an evident uneasiness about much of the work of his second prolific period which testifies to this perceived pressure. It cannot be said that the books which he went on to produce are inferior in quality to his earlier works, because he had learned enough about literary craftsmanship by then to carry him through his new endeavors successfully; nor can it be said that his imaginative fertility let him down. Nevertheless, some of the novels of this later period do strike one as being deliberately unambitious. Shaw is not by nature a fast writer, and presumably had not attained in 1975 the measure of commercial success that would have enabled him to set a less taxing target for himself, though it may be that the work ethic left over from his early socialization was also partly responsible for this insistence on and anxiety about productivity. Shaw, however, is not the first writer to have been disturbed by the demands of professionalism, and he will not be the last. He has the ability (and, perhaps more important in commercial terms, the growing reputation) to rise above these anxieties.

A Wreath of Stars (1976) is based on the marvellous premise that within our immediate cosmic environment there exist material bodies made up in such a way that they are insubstantial relative to commonplace matter; thus, two bodies might co-exist in the same space. The jargon borrowed from subatomic physics with which Shaw sustains this novel variant on the theme of parallel worlds is not altogether plausible, but that hardly seems to matter. In the story, the invention of a new type of plastic lens for augmenting night vision provides the means by which humans may see these alien entities. An "anti-neutrino world" passes spectacularly through the solar system, causing some alarm, though it is entirely impotent to affect *our* matter in any way at all. What it *does* affect, though, is an anti-neutrino planet that lurks within the Earth orbiting an anti-neutrino sun inside ours. This inner parallel-Earth is dragged away from the common center of gravity by the intruder, and miners in equatorial Africa, who use the new lenses to facilitate their work, are panicked by the periodic appearance in the lower galleries of "ghosts."

Boyce Ambrose travels from America to the emergent nation of Barandi to investigate the ghosts, having deduced the implications of the sightings. There he finds an ally in Gilbert Snook, an unwilling refugee trapped by circumstance into working as a teacher of English in the mining community. He also becomes involved with a female investigator sent by UNESCO to inquire into Barandi's use of foreign aid grants. Together, the three set out to make contact with the inhabitants of the parallel world, while Barandi's rulers play deadly political games that gradually involve and threaten them.

A Wreath of Stars has a tense, fast-paced narrative which—like the first part of *The Palace of Eternity*—undergoes an abrupt change of perspective as it reaches a sub-climax. The story is occasionally harsh, generally choosing to focus on the character and thoughts of the alienated Snook rather than the more sympathetic Ambrose, exaggerating his isolation in our world in order to lay the groundwork for his subsequent literal *alien*-ation, when he is metamorphosed into antineutrino flesh. The device which brings this transmogrification is, however, too plainly an arbitrary *deus ex machina* which completely undermines the already tenuous credibility of the story. There is much in the book to excite the reader, but the elements do not quite combine into a satisfactory coherent whole.

The second book which Shaw published in 1976 was his second collection, *Cosmic Kaleidoscope*, which brought together most of the stories published since the appearance of *Tomorrow Lies in Ambush*, plus two original stories and some inferior material left over from earlier days. (The UK and U.S. editions of the collection differ slightly, as do the editions of *Tomorrow Lies in Ambush*, but the difference is insignificant.) The best of the light-hearted pieces in the book are "A Full Member of the Club" (1974), about the ultimate in status symbols and their effects upon those fortunate enough to own them, and the original "The Gioconda Caper," in which it is revealed at last why Leonardo da Vinci painted more than one (in fact, more than fifty) Mona Lisas. "Waltz of the Bodysnatchers" (1976), about a conspiracy to murder in a world where killers have to compensate their victims in an unusually literal manner, is also a very effective story. The second original story, "Skirmish on a Summer Morning," is a sober and unusual science fiction Western, complete with a classical gunfight, while the other notable piece in this collection played any way but for laughs is the slice-of-life story, "A Little Night Flying," about the difficulties faced by police patrolling a world where antigravity harnesses have given everyone the power of flight. As with *Tomorrow Lies in Ambush*, *Cosmic Kaleidoscope* is readable without being particularly impressive, and does not display Shaw's talents to their best advantage.

Medusa's Children, which was the first of Shaw's two novels published in 1977, is a tightly-packed adventure story. Like *A Wreath of Stars* it is based on a bold but rather implausible hypothesis. According to the story, the reason why periodic changes in Earth's mean surface temperature do not result in dramatic changes in sea level as the polar ice-caps grow and shrink, is that there are teleportation devices regulating the amount of water in the sea by piping the "excess" across space to ice-bound water planetoids orbiting the sun. Along with the water go fish, cephalopods, and even the occasional shipload of humans (one of the transmitters is in the Bermuda Triangle); thus, a tiny human colony survives beneath the surface of one of the planetolds, maintaining an astonishing and precarious existence. They scavenge for bubbles of air, and for ice to be melted into drinkable water, and live in the patched-up hulls of ancient vessels gathered together into a submarine village. They are threatened by disease, by carnivorous fish, and most of all by mutated giant squids, while at the center of their world lives the intelligent zoophyte Ka, which continually adopts new individuals of all species into its group mind.

The story is set in the future, when the world is slowly recovering from catastrophe. The Earth is growing colder and the teleportation devices have begun to transmit water back to the oceans. There thus arises a chance for the humans to be saved (though they do not know it, and have no knowledge of Earth at all); and also a chance for Ka to extend his dominion. Sea-farmer Hal Tarrant first realizes that something odd is happening when he discovers that his operation is being sabotaged by the mutated squid, and from then on the action does not relent for a second as plot and counterplot gradually fuse.

The improbabilities in the plot are legion, but Shaw weaves his various ideas together into an aesthetically-pleasing net, and as an imaginative adventure story *Medusa's Children* is entirely adequate. What is missing from it, though, is any kind of wider implication such as can be found in *Ground Zero Man* or *Orbitsville*; for the time being, Shaw was concentrating on pure entertainment. This was further emphasized by the book that followed *Medusa's Children* in 1977, *Who Goes Here?*

Who Goes Here? was the first story in which Shaw attempted to deploy his humorous gifts at novel length. The story is a sheer delight, smoothly-written and elegantly-plotted. Warren Peace joins the Space Legion in order to forget (forgetfulness is guaranteed by the induction procedure), but then begins to torture himself wondering what memories he had that he so desperately wanted to be rid of—a problem made acute by the fact that, by accident or design, he has forgotten *far* more than any of his new comrades. Eventually, he gets the chance to desert and to go in search of his lost past—and finds it, though not without considerable difficulty and the odd time-paradox or two. Though it has echoes of Harry Harrison's *Bill, the Galactic Hero*, Shaw's novel is not really satirical. It pokes innocent fun at a few SF *clichés* but is best regarded as pure comedy; it succeeds where so many other efforts fail by maintaining a strong and steady pace, and by never losing its shape—when all the puzzles are finally resolved, everything *fits*.

Neither *Medusa's Children* nor *Who Goes Here?* is disappointing at its own level. They do not seem to be rushed, and are by no means clumsy or careless in construction. They are, however, economical in more ways than one. Apart from the tidiness of their plotting (a virtue which should not be underestimated), they place no real strain on the author's abilities; they are literary confections, containing little in the way of food for thought.

The same is true, perhaps to an even greater extent, of *Ship of Strangers*, Shaw's van Vogtian fix-up novel cast in the mold of the latter's *The Voyage of the Space Beagle*. It puts together a few previously-written short stories and one new novella to tell a rather old-fashioned tale of interstellar exploration. The parts are clever, but the whole—understandably—lacks unity, and it seems to be directed very much at the SF purist who remembers *Astounding* with nostalgic fondness.

The best part of *Ship of Strangers* is the original section which concludes the book, in which the *Sarafand* gets lost and winds up in a volume of space which is rapidly contracting—a "dwindlar" which eventually carries the luckless starship with itself into a new continuum. There is one beautiful moment in the story when what appears to be a ghost begins to materialize inside the ship, emerging from the body of a dead crewman: a ghost whose true identity turns out to be more marvellous than anything any spiritualist ever dreamed of. Like its predecessors, *Ship of Strangers* is eminently readable, but conspicuously unambitious.

The second novel which Shaw published in 1978, however, marked a distinct change of pace, and took him back from ingenious playing with ideas to far more difficult literary endeavors. *Vertigo* is the same kind of novel as *One Million Tomorrows* and *Other Days, Other Eyes*, constructing with scrupulous attention to detail a near-future social world profoundly altered by a single innovation: the antigravity harness first displayed in "A Little Night Flying." *Vertigo* is a direct sequel to the earlier story, taking up the account of its policeman hero's attempt to recover his health and self-confidence after being badly injured in a fight to the death with an airborne outlaw.

The antigravity device which is the focal point of the novel has given human beings the power of individual flight. The invention is subject to a series of limitations which prevent more spectacular applications: it will not lift anything much heavier than a man. Shaw's careful analysis of the way such a device would affect everyday life gives the impression of thoroughness and great sensitivity—there is not an element of the background which seems out-of-place, and the descriptive passages are full of delicate touches. In its representation of the psychological and sociological consequences of the invention the novel is utterly convincing—a product of the finest imaginative craftsmanship.

Robert Hasson, the hero, has lost his nerve as well as health in the terrible fall which concluded "A Little Night Flying." He can no longer bear to fly—a phobia which attracts considerable social stigma. He is sent to Canada to recuperate, but becomes embroiled in a local conflict which escalates when a businessman starts a crusade against a gang of delinquent flyers. Hasson has to regain his competence in dealing with fraught social relationships, winning back his dominant position in the human pecking order, as a prelude to attempting to subvert the developing vendetta. Eventually, when things get out of hand, only he can bring them under control, but to do so he must fly again. The climax of the story is set in a burning building four hundred meters above ground level; here he must conquer his fears and recover the freedom which he has lost.

Because the plot of *Vertigo* is concerned with the actions of ordinary people involved with small-scale problems, it seems as natural as the background against which it is set, encouraging the illusion that the book is only marginally science-fictional. Unlike Sam Tallon or Jack Breton, Hasson has no opportunity to save the human race. No one is under threat but a few people who—arguably—fully deserve to suffer the consequences of their actions anyhow. Hasson, unlike Garrod in *Other Days, Other Eyes* or Carewe in *One Million Tomorrows*, has no special responsibility in respect of the crucial invention that has the power to transform society: he is merely one of the millions of men whose lives have been transformed. This displacement of the action from the "center" to the "periphery" certainly makes *Vertigo* seem more modest than its predecessors, but the fact that the crucial hypothesis is not paraded like a colored banner does not imply that it is any the less vital to the construction of the story. The matter-of-fact way in which the transformed world is described makes it familiar to the reader very quickly, but it is an insensitive reader indeed who mistakes this feeling of familiarity for a lack of imaginative ambition on the part of the writer. *Vertigo* presents a precise and authoritative account of the confrontation of ordinary people and the fulfillment of an ancient dream. It is about a new kind of freedom which, like all freedoms, has to be controlled and domesticated. Inevitably, the mundanity of air-traffic lanes and CG commuters seems to be a kind of betrayal of the dream (for the characters as well as for the more ambitiously-minded readers), but this is the undoubted fate of all new and hopeful technologies.

One of the key passages in the novel, which demonstrates yet again Shaw's ability to make telling points with great economy and sensitivity, is one in which Hasson remembers his own personal attempt to reclaim the transcendent promise which the achievement of flight seemed to offer. This is how Shaw describes the climax of his long upward journey:

> He had already climbed higher than most fliers even cared to
> think about, and the nameless hunger within him was slowly

abating. On the other hand, he had reached a dimensionless zone—once the domain of the big jets—and going on upwards into regions of darker blue seemed just as logical and natural as returning to the ancient kingdoms of men. With his head tilted back, and arms and legs trailing limply, Hasson continued his climb, his posture an unconscious echo of the one in which mediaeval artists depicted human souls ascending to heaven. A single point of light—possibly Venus—appeared in the aching purity above him, beckoning, and Hasson swam towards it.

His rate of ascent was decreasing with every minute, in inverse proportion to the drain on his power packs, but a further hour took him to an altitude of twenty-five kilometres. The world curved away beneath him in nacreous splendour. There was no visible movement anywhere, except for the hastening progression of needles across the dials on his chest panel. Hasson flew onwards.

At thirty kilometres above sea level he checked his instruments and saw that his upward movement had all but ceased. His CG field generator, with less and less invisible grist for its mills, was expending stored energy at a prodigious rate simply to keep him from falling. The only way in which he could gain more height would be to discard the dead power packs, but he had ruled that action out, and in any case the result would be of no great significance. He had done what he set out to do.

Hanging motionless in the icy blue solitude, poised on the threshold of space, Hasson gazed all about him and felt...*nothing*. There was no fear, no elation, no wonder, no sense of achievement, no communion with the cosmos—removed from the context of humanity he had lost his humanity.[4]

Juxtaposed with this remembrance, a mere few pages further on, is Hasson's brief commentary on the new tribalism of the aerial "youth culture"—the *weltanschauung* of the dangerous and anarchic night-flying gangs:

One of the difficulties Hasson had encountered in his years of police work was that all the arguments were emotional rather the intellectual. He had lost count of the occasions on which he had interviewed members of a group who had just seen one of their number smeared along the side of a building or sliced in two on a concrete pylon. In every case there had been an undercurrent of feeling, akin to dawn-time superstition and primitive magical beliefs, that the deceased had brought misfortune down on himself by violating the group's code of behaviour in some way. He had defied the leader's authority, or had betrayed a friend, or had shown he was losing his nerve.

The death was never attributed to the fact that the young flier had been breaking the law—because that would have opened the door to the notion that controls were necessary. The nocturnal rogue flier, the dark Icarus, was the folk hero of the age. At those times Hasson had begun to wonder if the whole concept of policing, of being responsible for others, was no longer valid.[5]

This observation is made while Hasson's spirits are very low; the climax of the book is a validation of "policing"—not so much in the narrow sense, but in the wider sense of collective responsibility and control. Yet it is, at the same time, Hasson's triumphant recovery of the freedom of the air, the recapture of that part of the dream which *is* real. Thus, Shaw shows us not only a technological innovation wholly integrated into a near-future lifestyle, but emphasizes strongly what much science fiction *de*-emphasizes: the necessity of a co-adaptation between technology and the lived-in world which preserves historical and social continuity while genuinely increasing the range of human endeavor and experience.

Though *The Palace of Eternity*, *Other Days, Other Eyes*, and *Orbitsville* might make their own claims on different grounds, there are several good reasons for regarding *Vertigo* as Shaw's best book. It displays his main strengths as a serious writer: his ability to calculate the implications of his hypotheses and display them convincingly; and his ability to create a lived-in world different from our own. It is a novel which clearly offers the promise of better things to come.

Dagger of the Mind, published in 1979, is an experiment in suspense—a minor work in the Shaw canon, but one developed with the same scrupulous care that is typical of his best work.

The novel's central character is John Redpath, an epileptic who has found temporary social stability in working for a research institution in a small town. He is taking drugs which are supposed to stimulate his latent telepathic ability, and when he becomes involved in a chain of surreal and extremely disturbing experiences he does not know quite what to make of them. His desperate attempt to work through the web of hallucination to a coherent solution is confused by his uneasy romantic relationship with the story heroine, and the lack of self-confidence which arises from his illness.

Psychological dramas of this kind actually tend to be rather more disturbing when the stories are set in an apparently-mundane context, where the suspicion of insanity and the threat of the irrational seem more powerful. In a science fiction novel unusual events can happen routinely, and there is a massive apparatus of conventions which can be invoked in order to rationalize them into some kind of coherent pattern. Shaw artfully plays off his moments of *grand guignol* against the minutiae of everyday life, but the reader always has the advantage of knowing that a science-fictional resolution will set everything "to rights." The greatest dislocation of expectation happens, in fact, when Redpath begins behaving in a manner rather different from the way that protagonists in novels usually behave.

The gap in Shaw's production after *Dagger of the Mind* is associated with his undertaking to write the text of an imaginary travelogue to be published with illustrations by David Hardy; this seems to have absorbed more creative energy than he bargained for. Thus, *Dagger of the Mind*, if it does not actually mark the end of a distinct phase in Shaw's work, nevertheless provides a convenient point for a commentary on that work to be suspended. There remain to be mentioned only the short stories which Shaw has published since *Cosmic Kaleidoscope*, of which the best are the ingenious SF detective story, "Frost Animals" (1979), the Sheckleyesque "In the Hereafter Hilton" (1980), and what is perhaps the funniest of all his comic pieces, "Cottage of Eternity" (1979). Like *A Wreath of Stars*, "Cottage of Eternity" makes clever use of the jargon of subatomic physics, and like *The Palace of Eternity* it provides a science-fictional rationalization of life-after-death; but here the ingenuity is devoted to the generous development of humorous absurdity. Shaw apparently derives a good deal of pleasure from his shorter pieces—he once told me that he would rather be a short story writer than a novelist if the marketplace would permit it; but with one exception his greater achievements by far have been longer works, and his novels to date are much more impressive than his collections of short stories. He has never written a "big" novel of the kind beloved by American publishers (and, it seems, by the American public), but in view of the fact that most very long novels are simply inflated from their due size by inconsequential padding, this is no bad thing. Shaw is by nature an economical writer, with a concise rhetorical style, and there would be little point in his attempting to follow fashion in this regard. His novels may test his skill and stamina to the extent that they make him feel uncomfortable, but in doing so they get the best out of him.

If we recall at this stage Shaw's manifesto for science fiction as an "escape to reality," and his notion of "fiction as algebra," it is appropriate to ask how close he comes to the fulfillment of his own promises. The problem with this particular apologia for SF is that it is so difficult to find examples which strike the right balance between imaginative extravagance and realism of presentation. Shaw has at least begun to show how the difficulties of achieving this balance might be overcome, and his attempts to live up to his manifesto have begun to make up for the dearth of good examples.

III.

REALISTIC ROMANCES

THE FANTASTIC FICTION OF EDGAR FAWCETT

Edgar Fawcett was born in New York in 1847. His father was an Englishman who became a prosperous merchant in New York; his mother was of American descent. He graduated from Columbia College in 1867 and received his M.A. three years later. He then became a gentleman of leisure and a man of letters, writing poetry, essays, plays, and novels. He was a prolific writer, publishing more than forty novels, seven volumes of poetry, and two verse dramas. One collection of his essays appeared, though others were published in periodicals, and five of his plays were produced in New York and Boston. In addition, he copyrighted many other manuscripts which were never actually published.

The public apparently remained indifferent to virtually all his work, and the reviewers frequently treated his work with contempt. As he was essentially a dilettante—he was never dependent upon such income as he received from his writing—his motivation was a desire for recognition and appreciation that was never fulfilled. He launched many bitter assaults against the critics, the reading public, and the publishers. Of the three, he considered the critics the most guilty, and he made war upon them with a fervor that has rarely been equalled, and was surpassed only by the occult writer, Marie Corelli. The alienation of their affections seems to have continued even after his death. Fawcett's entry in *The Dictionary of American Biography* (1931), written by Oral Sumner Coad, is icily uncharitable not only in its description of his work but also in its comments upon his life-history:

> His chief volumes of verse...reveal but a slender talent. A strained mode of expression and echoes of the major Victorians too often usurped the place of inspiration...
> It was as a novelist that Fawcett made his bulkiest contribution to the literature of the day. His volumes of fiction number approximately thirty-five, and with wearisome uniformity they reiterate one main theme...the amateurishness of Fawcett's plots, the woodenness of his characters, the dreary earnestness of his manner, and the monotony of his subjects are sufficient to justify Henry Stoddard's plaint: "Won't somebody please turn this Fawcett off?"...
> Whether from a sense of irritation at the contempt with which certain newspaper critics in New York treated his work, or from other cause, Fawcett at the age of fifty left America and took up his residence abroad. London was his home during his last years, and here, in bachelor quarters in the Chelsea district, he died after less than a week's illness.

He was not entirely without supporters, and his poetry in particular was praised by other writers, including Julian Hawthorne, James Russell Lowell, and—most effusively—William Dean Howells. Nor was the unpopularity of his prose works entirely attributable to literary shortcomings. It was his subject-matter as much as his style which tended to cause offense. The "one main theme" to which Coad refers (though it is far from being the *only* concern in his works) is the snobbery and artificiality of New York society and social life. By virtue of having money (and—slightly more important in some circles—an English father), Fawcett was able to move in relatively elevated social circles and to compare what he saw there with the various European versions of the *haut monde* which he observed during his travels. In many novels—the early *A Gentleman of Leisure* (1881) may stand as a prototype—his heroes conduct a running commentary upon the ills and evils of New York society, deploring the rigidity of its stratification, the arrogance and affectation of its cliques, and the way in which it apes the fashions of Europe. Coad concedes that "The picture thus drawn, allowing for the necessary exaggeration of satire, is not unveracious, especially in its presentation of the struggle between the old Dutch patricians and the new plutocrats." The project, however, was hardly calculated to win influential friends.

As well as his criticism of the social élite—which led him on occasion to voice socialist opinions—Fawcett was an ardent champion of agnosticism, and frequently wrote in scathing terms about the dogmas of orthodox religion. His volume of essays, *Agnosticism and Other Essays* (1889), carried an introduction by the famous freethinker and opponent of Christianity, Robert G. Ingersoll. The battle between religion and rationalism is another of his favorite themes, and forms the chief subject-matter of two long philosophical novels, *A Demoralizing Marriage* (1889) and *Outrageous Fortune* (1894). His partisanship in this battle can hardly have helped him win favor with the majority.

If his own generation was ungenerous in its treatment of Fawcett, posterity can hardly be said to have redeemed his reputation. At least in his own day he was something of a celebrity; ten years after his death he was quite forgotten. His works were never reprinted, and all of them faded into obscurity. In the more than eight decades that have elapsed since his death virtually no attention has been paid to the man or his work save for the efforts of Stanley R. Harrison, who produced a doctoral dissertation on Fawcett for the University of Michigan in 1964, to which was appended an edition of one of Fawcett's unpublished novels and a collection of his letters. The critical commentary was expanded and published as a monograph in 1972. Harrison claims for Fawcett no more than that he was an interesting minor writer of his period, who played an important role in "the literary movement that proved to be the breeding ground for the works of Hamlin Garland, Stephen Crane, Frank Norris, Jack London, and Theodore Dreiser"—*i.e.*, the tradition of American Realism and Naturalism.

Harrison says of Fawcett:

> Fawcett's novels, essays, poems, and plays offer an insight into the political corruption of his age, a commentary upon the existence of a plutocracy within a democratic nation, a feeling for the confusion created by new philosophical concepts, and a reaction to the consequences of scientific learning and progress. His works also provide a rare insight into the origin, philosophy, and esthetic development of literary Realism and Naturalism, and a significant view of the international theme in American literature,

as well they might, since these literary movements were themselves outgrowths of the wider intellectual currents of the time.

Harrison's interest in Fawcett is primarily concerned with his attempts at narrative realism, but he does observe that there was another side to Fawcett's work, reflected in a number of romantic melodramas. Harrison regards these as minor works, and to judge by his descriptions most of them are indeed devoid of interest; but at the end of the chapter on "Fawcett and Romance" he observes that Fawcett wrote three other "non-realistic novels," which he says "were not of a piece with the standard fare of his romances." He adds that "They were journeys into the mind, excursions into fantasy; each one is fresh, inventive, and certainly experimental for its time." Having said this, and dutifully summarized the plots of the three works to which he refers, Harrison passes on to matters which are of greater interest to him.

The group of works to which the three titles Harrison dubs "non-realistic" belong is, however, of considerable interest in its own right, for it reveals Fawcett's importance in connection with a literary tradition quite apart from the slowly-nourished growth of narrative realism. Like many European and American writers of the period who were interested in Realism, Fawcett retained an interest in a special kind of Romance: in a kind of Romantic writing which absorbed something of the outlook of Realism—a Romantic fiction transfigured by rationalism.

There are, in fact, five—perhaps six—published works by Fawcett which belong to the curious category set aside by Harrison. He names *Solarion* (1889), *The New Nero* (1893), and *The Ghost of Guy Thyrle* (1895). The other two confirmed titles are *Douglas Duane* (1887) and *A Romance of Two Brothers* (1891). Fawcett himself mentions in this connection a story called "The Great White Emerald," but this has so far proved elusive—it does not figure in Harrison's bibliography or any other that I have been able to check. It seems certain, however, that Fawcett wrote more works of this kind, for in the list of stories copyrighted by Fawcett but never published (which Harrison provides) are two unambiguous titles: *The Man from Mars* (1891) and *The Destruction of the Moon* (1892). Some of the other titles listed might belong to the category; *Was It a Ghost?* (1885) seems a likely candidate. It is not known at present whether manuscripts of these works survive. What *is* certain, however, is that Fawcett recognized these stories as belonging not only to a *distinct* type, but also to a *new* type. To the last and best of them, *The Ghost of Guy Thyrle*, he added an "epistolary proem" which is a kind of manifesto in justification of the species. The name of the addressee is represented only by a row of asterisks, but the message runs as follows:

> Do you remember how you once called a few former tales of mine ("Douglas Duane," "Solarion," "The Romance of Two Brothers," and perhaps also "The Great White Emerald") ghost-stories pure and simple? I then declared to you that I had never written a positive ghost-story in my life; and now, when I send you my "Ghost of Guy Thyrle," I am obstinate in repeating this assertion. Here, as in those other works, you will discern no truly "superstitious" element.... Perhaps I am only a poor pioneer, after all, in the direction of trying to write the modern wonder tale. It seems to me that this will never die till what we once called the Supernatural and now (so many of us!) call the Unknowable, dies as well. Mankind loves the marvellous; but his intelligence now rejects, in great measure, the marvellous unallied with sanity of

presentment. We may grant that final causes are still dark as of old, but we will not accept mere myth and fable clad in the guise of truth. Romance, pushed back from the grooves of exploitation in which it once so easily moved, seeks new paths, and persists in finding them. It must find them, if at all, among those dim regions which the torch of science has not yet bathed in full beams of discovery. Its visions and spectres and mysteries must there or nowhere abide. Whenever we have spoken together of realism, my friend, you will recall how I have always held that a few polemic writers are not decrying the romantic, but rather the artificial. Romance is a shadow cast by the unknown, and follows it with necessitous pursuit. It can only perish when human knowledge has reached omniscience. Till then it may alter with our mental progress in countless ways, but the two existences are really one. Books like "Zanoni" and "A Strange Story" thrilled us in earlier years. Nowadays we want a different kind of romanticism, a kind that accomodates itself more naturally to our intensified sceptic tastes. It is the actual, the tangible, the ordinary, the explained, that realism always respects. From the vague, the remote, the unusual, the problematic, it recoils. Yet frequently the two forces of realism and romanticism have met, as in Balzac's "Peau de Chagrin," which might be called a fairy-tale written by a materialist. To make our romances acceptable with the world of modern readers, we must clothe them in rationalistic raiment. So clothed, my friend, I should name them "realistic romances"— stories where the astonishing and peculiar are blent with the possible and accountable. They may be as wonderful as you will, but they must not touch on the mere flimsiness of miracle. They can be excessively improbable; but their improbability must be based upon scientific fact, and not upon fantastic, emotional, and purely imaginative groundwork. From this point of view I occasionally strive to prove my faith in the unperished charm and potency of romance...

What Fawcett produces here is a manifesto for a species of imaginative fiction specifically adapted to the world-view of committed agnostics; a prospectus for tales of wonder which will have no traffic with such superstitious ideas as agnosticism is dedicated to oppose. If the prospectus is taken as a prophecy, then it is a remarkably accurate one; since Fawcett's time there has indeed been a luxuriant growth of exactly such a genre as he describes. It is usually known as "science fiction," though the label carries various undesirable implications. H. G. Wells, who published his first important "realistic romance" in the same year that Fawcett published *The Ghost of Guy Thyrle*, referred to his efforts as "scientific romances"; some modern commentators favor the designation "speculative fiction." Whatever label is preferred, it is clear that all of them represent attempts to map out and establish the boundaries of the same imaginative territory.

The fact that Fawcett produced several examples of science fiction *avant la lettre* is not in itself remarkable. Many other writers of the period—and of earlier periods—had done the same; H. Bruce Franklin's annotated anthology *Future Perfect* (1966; rev. 1978) gives some idea of the range of such work. Nor can it be said that his work influenced others, at least so far as the present-day historian can detect. Though several other writers acquainted with Fawcett also wrote imaginative fiction, their works which have most in common with Fawcett's realistic romances were written before he began, and any influence must have flowed the other way.

Nevertheless, Fawcett's realistic romances are of interest for precisely the same reason that his realistic novels are of interest: they offer a special insight into one aspect of the social and intellectual climate of his day. They are products of their time, and could not have been written at any other time, though this does not prevent their being highly individualistic works. They belong to a rather curious subspecies of science fiction which was developed almost entirely by American writers (many of whom were known to Fawcett and most of whom were sympathetic to the ideas which he held), but within this subspecies they have certain unique and interesting features.

This subspecies consists of stories of mental aberration, and its unifying characteristic is a strong interest in the proto-science of pre-Freudian psychology. The leading propagandist for this new science was Herbert Spencer, but the American literary community had a special reason to take an interest in it, because the leading American scholar in the field was William James, brother of the novelist Henry James. It was William James who first realized the importance of mental aberrations and the contribution an understanding of such abnormalities might make to an understanding of the working of the ordinary mind. Imaginative fictions working with such themes include: *Elsie Venner* (1861) and *The Guardian Angel* (1867) by Oliver Wendell Holmes, *The Queen of Sheba* (1877) by Thomas Bailey Aldrich, *Archibald Malmaison* (1879) by Julian Hawthorne, *Dr. Heidenhoff's Process* (1880) by Edward Bellamy, *The Mystery of Evelyn Delorme* (1894) by Albert Bigelow Paine, and *The Mortgage on the Brain* (1905) by Vincent Harper. Some, though not all, of the stories in William Dean Howells's collections, *Questionable Shapes* (1903) and *Between the Dark and the Daylight* (1907) might be added to the list. (All the authors named here are American. Aldrich and Hawthorne were Fawcett's friends, and Howells praised his efforts. Harper was an arch-rationalist whose attacks on superstition and the doctrine of the immortality of the soul are similar to Fawcett's, though rather more fierce. Holmes, of course, was in his own right an important pioneer in the practical science of psychiatry; Bellamy eventually became the chief prophet of American socialism.)

All but one of Fawcett's realistic romances carry a frame story which permits the main narrative to be interpreted as the history of a mental aberration. The exception carries an epilogue which serves the same function. In one story the mental aberration interpretation is forced upon the reader as the true one, and it is interesting that it is this story whose main narrative includes no fantastic incidents. In all the other cases the reader seems free to choose whether the enclosed narratives are "true" or the product of hallucinations, though the implication usually favors the former. The unique feature of Fawcett's work—and its most interesting aspect—is the way that he uses the logic of mental aberration as a literary device to open the way for more extravagant fantasies which are themselves internally rationalized by references to new scientific discoveries.

At its crudest, this strategy would amount to nothing more than a slightly sophisticated version of the *cliché* by which authors of wild fantasies always retained the option of a return to normality, by having the protagonist wake up and declare everything that had gone before to be a dream. Though Fawcett's fiction is in certain respects crude, this is not one of them; even if the narratives are to be accepted as hallucinations, this cannot simply dispose of their content, for it is implicit even in this interpretation that everything must be rational and accountable. Thus, if the fantastic narratives are to be deemed mental aberrations, they still must have causes, and they still must have an internal logic which explains their structure and psychological function.

The principal interest of the other writers named above is in mental aberration *per se*: in its logic, effects, and possible cures. The novels cited are mostly case-histories. Even the least fantastic of Fawcett's realistic romances, however, goes one step beyond this fascination with mental aberration for its own sake to further contemplation of the possibilities and possible costs of progress. How this is accomplished will be shown by detailed consideration of the works themselves.

Before summarizing Fawcett's realistic romances, it will be helpful to fill in a little more detail concerning his attitudes and his intellectual background. This will help to explain certain eccentricities and failures of imagination, as well as illuminating the single most important question around which his imaginative fictions revolve.

Firstly, it should be noted that Fawcett had no education in science itself, nor did he ever seem inclined to acquire any instruction in hard science. He was fascinated by the *philosophy* of science, and by the significance of the "scientific revelation," but of actual physics, chemistry, and biology he knew very little. This was a severe handicap in constructing the jargon of apology by which his enclosed narratives made their claims to plausibility. This handicap ruined his chances of becoming a really influential or innovative writer of realistic romances—he lacked the kind of credentials which the likes of H. G. Wells brought to the task. It is entirely in keeping with his character that he was able to write such a clear and concise manifesto for a *genre* without really having the equipment to put it into practice. The imaginative scope of *The Ghost of Guy Thyrle* deserves praise, but it must be admitted that it betrays a very primitive understanding of science.

Secondly, it is helpful to specify a little more exactly just who his intellectual heroes were, because he inherits some of the peculiarities of their thought. Foremost among them appears to have been Herbert Spencer, from whom he borrowed his strong emphasis on hereditary factors in psychology and his preoccupation with intellectual evolution. Spencer is commemorated in one of the sonnets in Fawcett's first important collection of poems, *Fantasy and Passion* (1878), where he is to be found in rather odd company (there are nine other admiring sonnets, addressed to eight writers and one artist: Poe, Whittier, Thackeray, Dickens, Keats, Dumas *père*, Hans Christian Andersen, Doré, and Baudelaire). Spencer is there described as "A spacious-brained arch-enemy of lies," and it is said of him that "His intellect is a palace...where...Calm Science walks, like some majestic queen!"

Spencer is often named in the realistic romances as a paradigm of philosophical virtue. Usually the names of other philosophers are sprinkled about with a gay abandon which suggests slight acquaintance with their ideas—references to Kant and Hegel seem to be mere name-dropping—but Fawcett appears to have found a certain sympathy with Schopenhauer. Douglas Duane refers to him as "the great Schopenhauer," and approves of his conclusions while disapproving of his aprioristic method (comparing him unfavorably, in this respect, with Spencer). It is not difficult to see how Schopenhauer managed to strike a resonant chord in Fawcett's imagination, for there is a determined pessimism about much of Fawcett's work—a kind of prideful brooding on the subject of death and the hopelessness of the myth of immortality. Fawcett, in his more philosophical moments, is much given to rhapsodies upon the futility of man's attempts to control his own destiny, and some of his plots are calculated to reveal the helplessness of individuals caught between the determinism of their heredity on the one hand, and the eccentric vicissitudes of chance on the other. Given this, it is not surprising that much of his realism and naturalism recalls the doctrines of Émile Zola rather than those of William Dean Howells. Again, his talents were not up to the task of putting the prospectus into operation in a convincing manner, but such novels as *A Man's Will* (1888) and *The Evil That Men Do* (1889) seem to be attempts to imitate Zola.

Thirdly, it should be noted that for Fawcett, the conflict of religion and science had as its focal point the issue of the immortality of the soul. This question fascinated him, and he could not let it alone. The idea of immortality, although rejected as a "revealed truth," continually drew his attention both as a force within human affairs with real social consequences and as a phenomenon to be accounted for in terms of psychology. Fawcett's preoccupation with mortality is particularly evident in his poetry—it haunts the better poems in *Fantasy and Passion*, and has a curious pre-eminence in his one futuristic work, the poem "In the Year Ten Thousand" from *Songs of Doubt and Dream* (1891). This poem is a dialogue between two citizens of Manattia, who first look out upon their Utopian world and recall the horrors of its distant past and congratulate themselves on the awesome progress they have made; but their discussion takes a more somber turn when the first speaker reminds the second that men must still die. Fawcett's own attitude, which seems covertly ambivalent behind the screen of his committed skepticism, is adequately displayed by the argument which follows:

SECOND MANATTIAN

Invariably; but death
Brings not the anguish it of old would bring
To those that died before us. Rest and peace
Attend it, no reluctance, tremor or pain.
Long heed of laws fed vitally from health
Has made our ends as pangless as our births.
The imperial gifts of science have prevailed
So splendidly with our mortality
That death is but a natural falling asleep,
Involuntary and tranquil.

FIRST MANATTIAN

True, but time
Has ever stained our heaven with its dark threat.
Not death, but life, contains the unwillingness
To pass from earth, and science in vain hath sought
An answer to the eternal questions—*Whence,
Whither, and For What Purpose?* All we gain
Still melts to loss; we build our hope from dream,
Our joy upon illusion, our victory
Upon defeat...Hark how those long winds flute
There in the dusky foliage of the park.
Such voices, murmuring large below the night,
Seem ever to my fancy as if they told
The inscrutability of destiny,
The blank futility of all search—perchance
The irony of that nothingness which lies
Beyond its hardiest effort.

51

SECOND MANATTIAN

Hush! these words
Are chaff that even the winds whereof you prate
Should whirl as dry leaves to the oblivion
Their levity doth tempt! Already in way
That might seem miracle if less firm through fact,
Hath science plucked from nature lore whose worth
Madness alone dares doubt. As yet, I allow,
With all her grandeur of accomplishment
She hath not pierced beyond matter; but who knows
The hour apocalyptic when her eyes
May flash with tidings from infinitude?

FIRST MANATTIAN

Then, if she solves the enigma of the world
And steeps in sun all swathed in night till now,
Pushing that knowledge from whose gradual gain
Our thirst hath drunk so deeply, till she cleaves
Finality with it, and at last lays bare
The absolute,—then, brother and friend, I ask
May she not tell us that we merely die,
That immortality is a myth of sense,
That God...?

SECOND MANATTIAN

Your voice breaks...let me clasp your hand!
Well, well, so be it, if so she tells. At least
We live our lives out duteously till death,
We on this one mean orb, whose radiant mates
Throb swarming in the heaven our glance may roam.
Whatever message may be brought to us,
Or to the generations following us,
Let this one thought burn rich with self-content:
We live our lives out duteously till death.
                              (A silence.)

FIRST MANATTIAN

'Tis a grand thought, but it is not enough!
In spite of all our world hath been and done,
Its glorious evolution from the low
Sheer to the lofty, I, individual, I,
An entity and a personality,
Desire, long, yearn...

SECOND MANATTIAN

Nay, brother, *you alone!*
Are there not millions like you!

FIRST MANATTIAN (*with self-reproach*)

Pardon me!
(*After another longer silence.*)

What subtler music those winds whisper now!..
'Tis even as if they had forsworn to breathe
Despair, and dreamed, however dubiously,
Of some faint hope!..[1]

In the final lines of the poem the reader learns that there may indeed be hope that the final mystery can be penetrated, for that very evening in Manattia there will be received the first message from the planet Mars. Having leaped ten thousand years into the future, though, Fawcett hesitates to venture one more day; his agnosticism would not permit him to beg that most crucial of questions by anticipating what the Martians might have to say upon the subject. When he could excuse himself with the possibility that his statement might be the result of a character's hallucination, however, he showed no such reluctance: Douglas Duane and Guy Thyrle are permitted to discover at least some solutions to the great mysteries.

Fawcett's first realistic romance, *Douglas Duane*, appeared in *Lippincott's Magazine* for April 1887. This magazine published a novel in every issue, including a separate title page so that the novels might be extracted and bound up as independent entities. *Douglas Duane* is actually rather short for a novel, running approximately 30,000 words.

The story begins when an old woman runs on to a New York street crying "Murder!" She tells a detective, Ford Fairleigh, that a Mr. Floyd Demotte has shot himself and his wife. Fairleigh discovers that Mrs. Demotte is, indeed, dead, but that Demotte himself is still alive and might still be saved. While this matter hangs in the balance, Fairleigh attempts to investigate the crime, but is handicapped by a lack of evidence as to motivation. The old lady tells him that before the incident she heard Demotte mention the name of Douglas Duane, his friend of earlier days, but Duane has been missing for some time.

Fairleigh discusses the case with his friend Hiram Payne, who suggests that Duane must have been Mrs. Demotte's lover. Fairleigh prefers the hypothesis that Demotte has gone mad, and that he shot his wife as a result of some delusion. (Much of the dialogue between Fairleigh and Payne consists of digressions which intrude social criticism into the story—there are bitter remarks about electoral justice and the life-chances of talented young men prevented from rising within the social hierarchy.)

Demotte recovers from his injuries, but goes from the hospital into a mental asylum where he eventually dies, though not before writing a remarkable story in explanation of what he has done. In his manuscript the injured man claims that he is not Demotte at all, but is the *persona* of Douglas Duane transferred into Demotte's physical *corpus*.

Duane begins by recalling his youth, when he was taken to Europe in order to attend Heidelberg University, where his father—a committed rationalist—believed that he would receive a better education than any available in America. Of his father, Duane says: "Thanks to his influence, I faced the dogmas and platitudes of daily existence with a prepared antagonism."[2]

This "prepared antagonism," however, has the effect of alienating him from his fellows and making him relentlessly cynical. In his intelligence and his realistic attitude to science he surpasses even his teachers:

> Demonstrative, exact thinking, the placid and patient search
> after physical law, the agnostic if not the atheistic way of regard-
> ing all final causes, and the fixed creed that mortal intelligence
> could never pierce beyond defiant boundaries of matter itself while
> very sensibly hoping for large realms of material enlightenment in
> the future—these considerations and assurances held a prodigious
> rule and influence over my daily life.[3]

When Duane's father dies, however, he returns to America to claim his inheritance and to enter society. He quickly falls into disfavor because of his unconventionality (he wears his hair long!), but continues to move in fashionable circles in a somewhat detached fashion. He makes one firm friendship, with Floyd Demotte, though the two men seem to have little in common. They debate metaphysical issues, with Duane taking a hard materialist line that Demotte cannot accept. Duane seems almost to despise Demotte for this weakness and for the fact that he is a book-collector who does not read. Duane, meanwhile, has his own laboratory, where he is pursuing research into the physical basis of mental phenomena—he is conducting an analysis of human will and action in terms of electromagnetic forces and impulses.

Demotte and Duane fall in love with the same girl, Millicent Hadley, but Duane's feelings are slightly confused. He prides himself on his own lack of emotionality, and he also knows that Demotte is a passionately jealous man. He determines to keep his own feelings secret when he concludes that Millicent prefers Demotte, but cannot help being embittered by Demotte's insensitivity, and becomes very miserable as his secret and hopeless passion grows. When Demotte and Millicent marry, Duane forces himself to attend the wedding and play the part of a true friend, but finds the effort agonizing. (He has already contemplated suicide, but has been held back by a visionary inspiration which promises him success in his work.) Demotte's jealousy, however, leads him to isolate Millicent from the society of others, so that she too becomes gradually miserable.

Meanwhile, Duane's research yields its fruits. He discovers that "identity" is reducible to a characteristic "charge" of electricity, and that if one *corpus* is deprived of its own charge another may be transmitted into it. Though his experiments are with plants, he does not doubt that the process will work even with human beings, and he quickly sees the possibility that he might secretly take the place of the man who has everything he desires, by dislodging Demotte's personality and substituting his own. He sets this idea aside, however.

Millicent confesses her unhappiness to Duane, and asks him if he will come to live in Demotte's house. Duane dares not accept, but tries to persuade Demotte to allow Millicent more freedom. Demotte tries, but the compromise soon becomes intolerable to them both. Again they appeal to Duane to live with them, and he accepts, knowing that it will lead to disaster. He confesses his love to Millicent and immediately leaves for Washington. She forgives him, but this only intensifies his misery, and Demotte's continued unawareness of the true facts of the situation finally goads Duane to action.

Duane disguises himself and stages his disappearance, returning secretly to New York. There he lures Demotte to his lodgings, electrocutes him, and uses his machine to project his own *persona* into the deactivated body.

While, as it were, in transit between bodies, Duane's soul experiences a crucial vision which penetrates beyond the material world that he had considered to be the limit of human knowledge:

> Strangely enough, after what seemed a short interval of frightful pain, I had no sensation of death. I seemed to be flying through infinite space, and yet my feeling of relief was exquisite. I had suffered untold tortures, but I was now entirely at peace. The driving and rending, the bursting and shattering of my brain had ended. Immeasurable visions, as of enormous planets swinging round enormous suns, and seen with an eye to which the eye of normal sight is contemptibly feeble, had rushed upon me. It was with me as though space had laid bare all her ethereal strongholds of glittering secrets. The feeling of disembodiment, of volatility, of splendid untrammelled liberty, was a rapture no language can portray. Time, as I now deduce, could no longer either measure or concern my transports. I had passed completely out of time. It did not occur to me (how should it?) that I was *still I*, and that the vital principle which I had so firmly believed an unconscious force when freed from material bonds could not only be and think but could be sublimely and think miraculously. And yet I was aware that I still lived, a naked soul, an essence of deathless intelligence and glorious capacity. The answers to a thousand mysteries of life, of nature, of science, of instinct, of religion, of even deity itself, shone before me in luminous and magnificent revelation. The problem of human suffering was no more a vexation; it had become lucidly solved. The whereas, the whither and the wherefore both of mankind and of all creation—those riddles which have tortured philosophy for so many futile centuries—were as plain to my comprehension as the radiant wheeling spheres which I gazed on were plain to my rarefied and emancipated vision. The universe had eloquently and irrefutably explained itself. My past scepticism, pessimism and negation had shrivelled to nothingness, as dry leaves could do if dropped into the white blinding fire of a furnace. But existence was not merely a divine expansion, possession and acceptance of the loftiest spiritual joy. It was more; it was a sacred fellowship with eternity—and eternity, like matter, beamed on me denuded of the least conceivable vagueness. Every perished or sentient creed of the world stretched before me as links in one immense necessary chain of circumstance. I saw atheism as it had been and as it still was, and neither condemned nor approved it; I simply understood its cause, its use, its meaning. I saw the long passionate drama of inextinguishable faith enacted throughout mankind here on my own little planet (and what an atom our globe looked among the grandeurs of other millions of globes!) and neither pitied martyr-

dom nor regretted persecution; both were effects and events of a development whose origin and terminus transcended inquiry.

But abruptly, in the midst of this noble and seraphic exaltation, this piercing and triumphant omniscience, a shade, a chill, a blight, fell upon me. I cannot put in words what I felt. It was not so much a realization of my freed and immortal personality being unfit for the exquisite happiness I had thus far enjoyed as it was a burdening, horrifying conception of my having deliberately flung aside and even murdered impulses of right in my past life by conniving at the death of a fellow-creature. All the unutterable beauty and brilliancy of my encompassments took suddenly an accusative aspect. The lights of the great lovely stars yet burned all about me, and shapes of untold harmony and grace yet floated on every side of me, but a darkness—or something that I can call by no other name than darkness, though it was not what we mean on earth by that word—had crept with a fleet and fearful stealth between my perceptions and the enchanting prospects I observed.... It seemed to me that a wild cry of supplication and of anguish now broke from my lips. "*My sin! my sin!*" I moaned, or seemed to moan. And at the same instant the blackness of that sin grew a close-encircling gloom and horror.... The effulgence and majesty of my surroundings faded.... The universality of knowledge which had in my mind died into an ignorance that left only a pathos of dim memory behind it, faint as the trail of a dying meteor in the dusky paths of heaven. And then came night, dense, weightsome, ineludible, befogging thought, that seemed to flicker and struggle like the blown flame of a candle before extinction leaps on it....[4]

This all takes two minutes, while the experiment succeeds and Duane finds himself "a murderer prisoned till death *within the shape of the being he had murdered!*"

It hardly needs pointing out that the revelation here vouchsafed to Douglas Duane would have delighted the First Manattian of ten thousand years hence. Here a man is discovering by means of scientific innovation exactly what the positivist philosophy declares to be unknowable. All that the march of intellect has obliterated from the reservoirs of religious faith is here restored as an aspect of future progress. The immortality of the soul is empirically demonstrated, perception is so wonderfully enhanced that nothing lies hidden from its curiosity, and even the moral order of things is carefully preserved as Duane's disembodied soul is soaked by universal conscience.

There is clear evidence here of a desperate desire which infected many nineteenth-century rationalists, to have their intellectual cake and eat it too. On the one hand, they attacked believers for accepting without true warrant a host of comforting beliefs, while at the same time hoping that the march of science might eventually provide a new and trustworthy warrant for an equally convenient set. Fawcett here reveals a certain imaginative kinship with the various scientists who were attracted by the supposed empirical evidence underlying spiritualist beliefs, and there is some evidence in this passage and others that he had read and had been impressed by Camille Flammarion's *Stories of Infinity*, which had appeared in an American edition in 1873. (I shall return to this point later.)

It is worth noting now that it is only in this first realistic romance that Fawcett offered to his protagonist a vision as complete and clear as this one. Even with the ambivalence conferred upon it by the possibility that it is a mere hallucination, it represents too definite a transgression of the basic principle of agnosticism—that the matters with which the revelation deals are in principle unknowable. Guy Thyrle embarks upon a much longer voyage into the unknown, but accomplishes far less in terms of an understanding of the nature and purpose of creation.

In the story, Duane's moment of terror and shame ebbs once he is again incarnate, and he sets off to Demotte's home, carrying a pistol with which he intends to kill himself should his loved one reject him. Millicent quickly realizes that he is not her husband, and she identifies him in spite of the apparent impossibility of her realization. Her terror overwhelms him as he realizes that the situation is hopeless; he shoots her and then himself in the hope that their souls may set out together into the eternity which he has glimpsed.

Neither Fairleigh nor Payne can accept the truth of what they read in this manuscript, and the conclusion of *their* story deals with Fairleigh's attempt to find corroborative evidence. Fairleigh has tried to find the apartment where Duane claims to have committed his crime, but has failed. A building destroyed by fire, however, *may* have been the one, so the failure is not conclusive evidence of the falseness of the story; and the fact remains, of course, that Douglas Duane's body—tenanted or untenanted—is still missing.

Solarion, which appeared in *Lippincott's Magazine* in September 1889, is even shorter than *Douglas Duane*, being hardly above 20,000 words, but it is by no means the least of the realistic romances. In terms of literary quality, it stands clearly second in the hierarchy, behind *The Ghost of Guy Thyrle*, and is a remarkably original work.

The frame-narrative of *Solarion* is of no importance in itself, but simply exists in order to cast doubt on the authenticity of the main story, which is told by Kenneth Stafford to Hugh Brookstayne. Brookstayne is a neurophysiologist who encounters Stafford—a man whose face has been half-destroyed by a dog—while in retreat in Switzerland. Brookstayne believes that Stafford's story is the result of a mental aberration brought on by his terrible experience.

Stafford seems to be in many ways another, but more moderate, version of Douglas Duane. As a youth he is rather effeminate, but harbors strong positivist leanings. He proves the fakery employed by a medium at a seance arranged by his mother and his Aunt Aurelia. Aurelia marries a man named Effingham, whose daughter Celia attracts Stafford considerably, but Stafford cannot spark a romance between them. It is little consolation that his rival for her love, Caryl Drayton, fares no better.

Following his mother's death, Stafford goes, as Douglas Duane did, to Germany, where he studies science in the same devoted and hard-headed fashion. Brookstayne, who is relaying Stafford's story to the reader, observes that:

> He had a rooted and inherent distrust of eloquence, and it gradually grew upon him that oratory as an art was one of the most harmful enemies of civilization. The deeper he plunged into science the more potently he was convinced of how its lustral waters cleansed the mind from every form of parasitic and clogging impediment. "I live," he once announced to a throng of intimates, "in search of nothing except the actual. Progress has for centuries lost untold opportunities, through her hospitality toward imagination. All dreams are a disease; the really healthful sleep has none.

It has often occurred to me that mankind now suffers from an immense and distracting toothache, called religion."[5]

Like Duane, Stafford is courageous in the face of the uncertainties which the positivist outlook necessitates, and is unworried by the thought that death might be final. He argues that death is not to be feared: "the dark slaves of oblivion wait upon us there; they are better than the loveliest houries; they can never be corrupted, for the simple reason that they are corruption itself." There follow the usual token references to various philosophers, including "the incomparable Spencer" and "the great Buckle," and Stafford goes so far as to quote a long section from Darwin's *Origin of Species* concerning the origin of life, expressing a special admiration for it. (Interestingly, Fawcett never mentions Ernst Mach, the German father of the positivist crusade.)

On leaving Berlin, Stafford travels to Strasbourg to see Conrad Klotz, the author of a treatise on electricity which was recalled because Klotz feared the consequences of its publication. Stafford impresses the old man, who is dying, and Klotz entrusts his manuscript to Stafford after accepting his word that he will destroy it. Stafford, of course, breaks his word and carries the treatise home with him to the U.S., determined to further the cause of science with its aid.

Back home, he renews his acquaintance with Caryl Drayton, now an Oxford-educated gentleman of leisure. He falls in love with Celia again, but she remains indifferent to him, and eventually embarks on a trip to Europe with her father and Stafford's aunt. Stafford then throws himself wholeheartedly—even obsessively—into his work.

Klotz's treatise concerns the subject of accelerated evolution by electrical stimulation, and Stafford begins his work with a bitch called Elsa, who soon produces a remarkably handsome puppy which Stafford calls Solarion. Taking his notion of evolution from Spencer, Fawcett construes the term mainly as growth in intelligence, and Solarion does indeed turn out to have remarkably-augmented intelligence. Stafford has doubts about his work—Brookstayne observes that his researches "were overshadowed by a terrible sarcasm of incompleteness"—but carries on regardless. Six years pass without a glimpse of Celia, but he consoles himself with the thought that at least Solarion is loyal and always close by.

Stafford feels that the crucial moment in his endeavor will be the experiment that will give Solarion speech, and he approaches this moment with great trepidation:

As he entered his laboratory on the particular day in question, Kenneth felt as though he were indeed about to call spirits from the vasty deep. And well might he so have felt. Superstition is fasing from the earth, but while men live and awe is an emotion that may be quickened, some adequate substitute will not prove wanting. The Unknowable, as an element in science, will continually supply this; for until all final causes are comprehended, mystery must ever hide at the base of both human knowledge and endeavour. Here will lie all the ghosts of our future "Hamlets," the witches of our future "Macbeths." Electricity is not the only nimble and fiery demon to be summoned by unknown sorcerors from nature's unexplored and shadowy gulfs. Light, heat, optics, chemistry, physics, mineralogy, will all have their weird and perchance blood-curdling messages to deliver, and it may well be that aeronautics will surpass even these in grandeur and suggestiveness of tidings. People with "nerves" will possibly be as much afraid to look through one of our coming telescopes as if they were now requested to walk at midnight through a graveyard. The mysterious will go on holding its own, precisely as before. Though fable will have perished, a sense of the vague, the mighty, the occult, even the diabolic, will yet remain.[6]

This passage is interesting for several reasons. It is, of course, an earlier version of the statement issued in the proem to *The Ghost of Guy Thyrle*, but here it is not a prospectus for Romantic literature so much as an attitude to science itself. It is important to remember that this is not Stafford speaking, but Brookstayne, and the statement thus has a weight which one could not attribute to any statement made by Douglas Duane or to the narrative voices of *The New Nero* or *The Ghost of Guy Thyrle*, all of whom are specifically called in question as "reliable" informants. There is no question of Brookstayne's reliability, and though he is still a character in a story, the close alliance between his statement and one later made by Fawcett on his own behalf suggests that his attitude is one which Fawcett could at least take seriously.

What is remarkable about such a statement, issuing as it does from a supposed neurophysiologist and man of science, in a story written by a professed agnostic and champion of science, is its dreadful anxiety. The "messages" to be revealed by the developing sciences are to be "weird," even "blood-curdling." What we see through telescopes will frighten us if we are predisposed to fear. The as-yet-unfolded possibilities of science carry a sense of the occult and the diabolic.

The attitude is not new, of course—we find it in the direful fantasies of Hoffmann when "mechanicians" construct doom-laden automata, and we find it most conspicuously of all in Mary Shelley's *Frankenstein*—but it is a remarkable attitude to find in the work of an anti-religious agnostic and a militant disciple of progress. It is noticeable that no good ever comes from any of the discoveries made by scientists in Fawcett's realistic romances—no matter how beneficial they may seem in potential, their role within the stories is to bring disaster.

Solarion continues with the development of a most curious "eternal triangle." The experiment which is to give Solarion speech succeeds, and marks the beginning of a new phase in the relationship between Stafford and his dog:

> From that moment his feeling toward Solarion altered; it became in a manner parental, and yet touched by a spell still more solemn and august. Mere ordinary birth, like every other mysterious matter which constantly goes on occurring, has become a triteness to us all. But Solarion appeared as one who has been born in some way that is appallingly new, and Kenneth soon had the sense of standing toward him in terms of miraculous fatherhood.[7]

Solarion quickly learns that to Stafford he is only an experiment—though the previously-quoted passage suggests that Stafford is not being entirely honest in saying so—but Solarion has no hesitation in replying to this revelation that to him Stafford is everything: his one ward against loneliness, his one chance of happiness. Stafford's reaction to this is peculiar: he charges Solarion with being the ghost of Conrad Klotz and faints, but later repents his weakness. Subsequently, when Solarion again declares his love for Stafford, Stafford reciprocates:

I return that love with all *my* heart! A cold ambition, a fatal selfishness, may at first have begotten you, but now the feeling I bear toward you is full of tenderness, of sanctity! You shall always be to me the strongest and dearest link between myself and life. Indeed, I shall live only *for* you, and in the marvels of this mind that I have unlocked it will be my happiness to find the most vivid and unfailing interest![8]

Despite this new relationship, however, Solarion remains unconvinced of the propriety of his own existence. He begs Stafford to keep Klotz's secret, lest hundreds more beings like him should be created.

The plot quickly takes another turn as Celia returns to America following the drowning of her father and step-mother. The moment Stafford sees her his love for her is revived, but it still seems hopeless. Celia has now been twice engaged, once to an Italian prince and once to Drayton, but both engagements were broken off—Drayton has told Celia that she is incapable of love, and she relays this judgment to Stafford.

Stafford explains to Solarion that he loves Celia, and there follows a curious debate concerning the foundations of morality. Stafford argues (as a devout Spencerian would be likely to) that the evolution of intelligence has been parallelled by an "evolution of conduct"—*i.e.*, that there is a moral as well as an intellectual progress. Solarion disputes this by pointing out that Stafford is a contradiction of his own beliefs, easy prey to vulgar ambition.

Celia rejects Stafford, but on seeing Solarion she seems to fall in love with *him*. Solarion never speaks to Celia (or to anyone else save Stafford, confirming Brookstayne's belief that Solarion's supposed abilities were all a delusion of Stafford's), but she eventually begins to suspect that there is something unusual about him. Stafford gives Solarion to Celia, partly in order that Solarion may spy on Celia and Drayton on his behalf, but when Drayton reports that he will marry Celia in spite of the fact that Celia does not love him, Stafford demands Solarion's return. Solarion refuses to return to Stafford, charging him with being "the merest self-loving tyrant," and Stafford seems set to lose everything.

In the end, Stafford decides that Solarion must die for the hurt he has inflicted upon his maker, and tries to shoot the dog. Solarion, however, succeeds in mutilating Stafford before he dies, tearing out one eye and destroying that side of his face. With Caryl and Celia married, Stafford has no option but to become an anguished recluse, and it is thus that Brookstayne has found him. Brookstayne's own narrative ends on a false and rather disappointing note, as he tries to draw a moral from the tale in alleging that Conrad Klotz has been avenged, and that Stafford has paid with his insane hallucination the price of his broken word.

A Romance of Two Brothers is the least of Fawcett's realistic romances. Though it was published as a book, it is again only a novella, running approximately 36,000 words. A note at the end reveals that it was written in London and Paris between August and October 1890.

This is the one story in the group which has no frame narrative, and it begins directly with a description of the circumstances of one Egbert Maynard, who lives in England near Cambridge. Maynard is unhappily married to Georgina, the reason for their unhappiness being a philosophical incompatability: Maynard is an atheist, Georgina is devoutly religious. Georgina is the daughter of a parson, and considers that she was wooed under false pretences, as Maynard did not tell her of his lack of faith until after the wedding. They have two sons, Sylvan and Gerald.

One day, Maynard responds to his wife's despair at their poverty by telling her that he has made "an immense discovery" in the laboratory which will enrich the family and prove a great boon to mankind. It is "a new kind of electricity"—the liquefaction of "the eternal principle of life" which spreads through the universe. Effectively, it is the elixir of life, and will make men immune to death by disease or old age.

Georgina Maynard's response to this news is one of horror: she describes it as "a shameful revolt...against the sacred laws of God."

Maynard's health is not good: he is tubercular and fears that he might die before his work is complete. Though he has the elixir, it is highly unstable and he has great difficulty in controlling its volatility. He will not rest until he has stabilized the fluid, and has conducted an experiment in which it revives a wilting rosebush. Unfortunately, the effect is only temporary.

Maynard suffers a haemorrhage soon after his partly-successful experiment, and lies at the brink of death for some time. Though he does not recover his power of speech, he eventually manages to control his hand well enough to write, and directs his doctor, Ross Thorndyke, to bring him the fluid from his laboratory. Thorndyke finds it gone. By means of a great effort, Maynard writes out the formula of the elixir and the means by which it may be stabilized, couching it within a letter to his elder son. This he gives to Thorndyke, insisting that Thorndyke must pass it to Sylvan on the boy's twenty-fifth birthday. He confronts his wife and charges her with stealing the fluid; this she admits, and he dies accusing her of murder.

Georgina Maynard, much embittered, soon follows her husband to the grave. Before doing so, however, she exerts a powerful influence upon the ideas and attitudes of her elder son. Sylvan has health problems like his father, and decides not to enter the Church, but studies instead for the law, eventually being taken to New York by a patron in order to attend Columbia College. Gerald, meanwhile, falls more under the influence of Ross Thorndyke, and studies in England with a view to entering the medical profession.

Sylvan sends Gerald money to support him through his education, but cuts off this support when he increases his own responsibilities by marrying a girl named Lucia Fythian. Thorndyke, however, takes over the responsibility before sailing to New York in order to deliver Egbert Maynard's letter at the appropriate time. Sylvan seems to Thorndyke very like his mother, and Thorndyke pities his wife, who is growing dissatisfied with their somewhat ascetic and reclusive life-style. When the doctor visits the family again, Lucia tells him what Sylvan found in the letter. Thorndyke cannot believe that Maynard actually found the secret of immortality, but Lucia seems fascinated by the idea—though Sylvan, of course, adopts the same attitude as his mother, and refrains from destroying the paper only because of a promise he has made.

The formula eventually becomes the cause of much strife between Sylvan and Lucia. She wants him to show it to Gerald, but he refuses. It becomes the focal point of her dissatisfaction with her marriage, and the breaking-point of the relationship is reached when—after she has tried to steal the letter—Sylvan appears to burn the formula before her eyes. In fact, he has tricked her, but this seems of little consequence as she leaves the house, swearing never to return.

Gerald comes to America in order to study with a Chicago doctor, Cranford Clyde, though he hopes eventually to practice in New York. He visits Sylvan, and finds him in a sadly depressed state because of his wife's desertion. Repenting too late of his obstinacy, Sylvan shows the letter to Gerald, who is skeptical but in-.

terested. Gerald takes it back with him to Chicago, and shows it to Clyde, who tells him to test the process.

Gerald perfects the fluid, apparently overcoming the problem which had faced his father. He decides to test the elixir on a human subject, and asks Clyde to secure the corpse of a drowned man in order to test its revivifying powers to the full. The corpse which Clyde obtains is, in fact, a young and beautiful woman, and Gerald falls in love with her even while she still lies inert. The elixir restores her to life, but she is suffering from total amnesia. Gerald names her Perdita, and fascination with her leads him to set aside his experiments for a while. He is even untroubled when Clyde accidentally breaks the flask containing the elixir.

Clyde becomes anxious about Gerald's new obsession, and asks Thorndyke to come to New York, where they are now working. Thorndyke, however, is compelled to remain in Chicago to tend the victims of a great fire. In the meantime, Sylvan asks Gerald to surrender the formula, intending to destroy it, but Gerald refuses and the two brothers quarrel bitterly.

Perdita eventually agrees to marry Gerald, but as the clergyman is about to perform the ceremony Sylvan arrives at the house, claiming that detectives have seen his missing wife there. Perdita, of course, is Lucia, and on seeing Sylvan she remembers everything. She suffers a heart attack and dies (though the possibility exists that Gerald, like his father, had not truly overcome the temporariness of the elixir's revivifying effect). Gerald, grief-stricken and humiliated, finally hands the formula over to his brother, who carries through his intention of burning it.

In an epilogue to the story Thorndyke and Clyde discuss the strange affair. Thorndyke believes that the elixir never did work, and that Perdita/Lucia was never truly dead; Clyde is not so sure, but there remains no way to settle the issue as Gerald cannot re-create the formula. The tragedy has brought the two brothers together again, and they are now very devoted to one another, but their amity is soon to be interrupted, for Sylvan's poor health is giving way inexorably, and there is nothing in the world that can save him.

The story is slight by comparison with the two earlier realistic romances, and the later chapters seem rather hurried and clipped. Because the whole story is told from an author-omniscient viewpoint rather than through the medium of a narrator, it is much more difficult for Fawcett to create the essential atmosphere of ambiguity surrounding the discovery and its effects. It is all very well for Thorndyke to express his skepticism at the end, and had the reader had an account of the various important experiments second-hand it would have been possible to share his opinion, but it does seem as if the reader has been told explicitly that the elixir *does* work, even if less powerfully than intended. It appears that Fawcett set out to write an unambiguous science fiction story for once, but gradually became dissatisfied with the project. This may provide a partial explanation for the fact that his next realistic romance was quite unambiguous in the other direction: it is a straightforward tale of hallucination.

The New Nero is in some ways a bad book. The plot of its main narrative is woefully unconvincing, and the fact that it is revealed as an invention of its fictional narrator hardly excuses the fact. It is, indeed, conceivable that Fawcett wrote the enclosed narrative first as a kind of philosophical romance, realized its deficiencies, and then adapted it to enclosure within the frame as a method of side-stepping its inadequacies. It is noticeable that the economy of the earlier works is quite absent; if anything, the story seems rather heavily padded (the book is a full-length novel of some 80,000 or more words).

The frame narrative deals with a visit by a man named Fanshawe to his uncle, Dr. Theobald, at the latter's place of work—a lunatic asylum. Fanshawe has previously argued with his uncle about the possibility of sane men being committed to asylums (possibly by unscrupulous relatives), and Theobald has dismissed such anxieties as unworthy of consideration. "Sanity," says the doctor at one point, "is just as hard to conceal as insanity."

At first Fanshawe is struck by the apparent normality and placidity of the patients he sees, but Theobald explains that not all patients are so obliging; he leads Fanshawe into the "remoter regions" of his hospital, where Fanshawe is horrified by stereotyped madmen writhing in their strait-jackets like wild beasts.

Fanshawe inquires after a famous writer who has been confined to the asylum, one Fleming Lancewood. Lancewood is described as an author of imaginative fiction to rival Poe: "a master magician in the way of all weirdly imaginative fiction." Theobald says that Lancewood's fantasies were the result of addiction to morphine, though Fanshawe seems to prefer the more romantic hypothesis that the writer was crazed by grief following the death of his fiancée.

Theobald has to leave Fanshawe in order to attend to a patient, and the young man is approached by a stranger, "his haggard features cut in lines of poetic beauty," implying "both despondence and distress." This man tells him that he is a patient, but that he has no hope of recovery and release because he is not really mad. Nor does he seek release, for what he really wants is to be punished for his crimes. He begs Fanshawe to save him from his too-kindly imprisonment, and gives Fanshawe a manuscript which comprises his confession.

In the manuscript the stranger introduces himself as Harold Mountstuart, an Englishman born in "Devon of a good family, one of whose scions once demonstrated his worthiness by declining an earldom." Mountstuart claims to have killed seven people for the sake of gaining the family fortune—all of them his uncles and cousins (the plot is strongly reminiscent, in fact, of the famous Ealing comedy film *Kind Hearts and Coronets*, but is in deadly earnest). Mountstuart is quick to insist that his is "no merely lurid tale of vulgar assassination. It is rather one which exhibits crime, I should say, in the light of a subtle and picturesque art, like that of the lapidary, the silversmith, or the painter of ivory."[9]

Mountstuart, in the tradition of Douglas Duane, Kenneth Stafford, and Gerald Maynard, is converted to the cause of rationalism at an early age, upon picking up a volume of Euclid:

> Some sort of door seemed to have been opened in my mind. Reason, for the first time, vividly woke within my brain, and by the light it shed I seemed to gaze with new eyes upon all other forms of intellectual pursuit.[10]

Mountstuart is sent to Eton, but recalled temporarily when his sister Gladys dies of heart failure. He finds himself unable to weep at the sight of the body, and realizes that he has never felt the least sentiment or affection for anyone. He discovers himself to be "an abnormal creature, a flesh-and-blood monster," and reflects that "If the world knew me as I knew myself, it would shrink from me as one, in a psychic sense, leprous. For, co-existent with this coldness, I discovered that my nature abounded in what I can best define as ethical torpor."[11] Other people, however, do not shrink from him, and he finds it easy enough to be popular with almost everyone.

Naturally, Mountstuart has no faith in God, and professes to regard life as "the most empty and aimless of travesties," and he becomes fascinated by the paradoxicality of his own existential situation. Rationalism, he is firmly convinced, represents a great advance in human affairs—a vital stage in intellectual evolution—but in him it has produced a monster: clever, clinical, and conscienceless. The accusation which Solarion threw at Kenneth Stafford Mountstuart hurls at himself again and again: he is a product of intellectual progress without moral progress. Because of his lack of feeling, agnosticism has produced in him not a sage but a killer.

Mountstuart is a great success at Cambridge, being both brilliant and popular. He considers making an advantageous marriage, but finds the thought of union with a woman nauseating. His mother at one point suggests to him that in a marriage it is not actually necessary for both partners to be in love, and he retorts by asking her whether this was true of her own marriage. She replies that in fact she *was* fond of his father (now deceased), but has to admit that she was not uninfluenced by the fact that at the time he seemed the likely heir to half a million pounds. Her husband had two elder brothers, but both seemed to be confirmed bachelors, and it seemed likely that Harold's father would be made the heir as head of the one branch of the family likely to continue. Unfortunately, both elder brothers had married late in life and produced children, so that now no less than seven people stand between Harold and the half million. Harold immediately forgets the thought of marriage which provoked the discussion, and becomes fascinated instead with the idea of murdering his way to the fortune.

At first he sets aside this notion as an absurdity, but his love of luxury goes beyond his rather limited means, and after inheriting the small Devon estate of Dyandotte following his mother's death he soon begins to make plans. He makes his first move when he goes to stay for a while with the present holder of the fortune, his uncle Malcolm. Malcolm has a habit of reading in bed by candlelight, and it is not too difficult to drug him one night and set his bedchamber aflame, rigging the whole matter to look like an accident.

The success of the first murder fills Mountstuart with a sense of destiny, and once his initial exaltation has faded he sets about his next step with calm resolve. His main problem is to avoid suspicion, and so he determines to have someone else hanged for his next murder. Egerton, Malcolm's son, provides him with his opportunity when he impregnates the daughter of his gamekeeper. Mountstuart, disguised as an Indian, eavesdrops on a meeting between Egerton and the girl's brother, and shoots Egerton while a quarrel is in progress, putting the gamekeeper's son very firmly in the frame.

Mountstuart comforts Egerton's sister Blanche, and it soon becomes apparent that if he wished to, he could marry her. He contemplates this course of action, but in the end rejects it. She has a dog of whom she is very fond, and one day the dog goes mad. It bites her, and the wound has to be cauterized. Mountstuart, discovering that the dog has rabies, makes a salve from its saliva, and gives this to Blanche to soothe the burn. Soon afterwards, he is summoned back to her bedside to watch her die an agonizing death. Everyone else, of course, assumes that she was infected by the initial bite—the reader is left to wonder how Mountstuart can possibly have known that she was not.

The second uncle and his family are very different from the first, being with one exception monstrously unpleasant. Cecil, the next inheritor of the cursed half-million, is simply coarse and anti-social, but his two elder children are loathsome. The boy, Angus, is physically deformed and inordinately fond of reptiles, while his sister Edna is jealous and malicious almost to the point of insanity—she persecutes her innocent sister Olive to the point where Olive must be sent to a relative in Canada to protect her.

Cecil is addicted to tobacco and already suffering severe physical symptoms as a result—it is an easy matter for Mountstuart to poison him with pure nicotine. Unfortunately, Edna witnesses the crime and denounces him for it, but her known maliciousness and the fact that the autopsy reveals no suspicious substances in the body result in her evidence being discounted. Nevertheless, Mountstuart decides that she must be next to go, and he persuades her long-suffering governess to take revenge upon her with prussic acid, poisoning herself immediately afterwards. After this, Mountstuart makes a close friend of Angus, whose only other friend is a large anaconda named Caligula. Mountstuart commits the most bizarre of all his murders by intoxicating the snake with pure alcohol so that it crushes Angus within its coils. Mountstuart then tries to kill the snake, but is unfortunate enough to fracture his own skull when the chamber of his pistol explodes.

Once recovered from this injury, Mountstuart sets off for Canada to carry news to Olive of the tragic fate of her kindred. His intention to murder her, and thus come into possession of the half-milllon, dies quickly once he has seen her; for the first time feeling is awakened within him, and he falls in love. He plans to marry her, but is unexpectedly confounded by her jealous friend, Roberta Stirling. Olive rejects Roberta when she slanders Mountstuart, but Roberta swears that she will prove that Mountstuart is evil in order to reclaim her friend. Mountstuart, knowing only too well how much there is that might be proved, resolves to murder her in order to secure his happiness. He steals up on her one evening as she stands on a cliff close to Niagara Falls, and prepares to push her to her doom, but while he moves to take up his position her place is taken by Olive, and he does not realize until too late that he has made an appalling error.

To his surprise, however, when grief leads him to confess everything, no one will believe him. It is said that all his murders are the figments of a deranged mind, and that even his identity is in question. Thus, though he longs only for due punishment, he finds himself confined to Dr. Theobald's asylum as a result of an imaginary delusion.

The story Mountstuart tells is so preposterous that the reader has great difficulty in sympathizing with Fanshawe, who believes that the manuscript does indeed prove the sanity of author. Most people would reach the opposite conclusion, and the verdict of common sense is for once confirmed when Dr. Theobald (surely to no one's surprise) explains that "Mountstuart" is actually Fleming Lancewood.

What is interesting about the story—and what really qualifies it as a realistic romance—is primarily Harold Mountstuart's commitment to explaining himself. He seems obsessed with the business of analyzing his own character, explaining himself as the product of an unfortunate combination of defective heredity and the intellectual environment into which chance delivered him:

> Often I would seek to analyse the cold depth of a disposition and temperament so different from all with which I came into contact. Repeatedly, at these times, the answer addressed me. I was the unhappy and unholy result of modern skepticism. I believed in nothing and comprehended that morality was only a utilitarian selection, a product of expediency, which had worked itself out into our present system of right and wrong after millions of centuries—from that shadowy period, indeed, when man had just ceased to be an ape until his slow progression had at last developed intellects of the finest and sturdiest fiber. This recognition, which to so many would have been a revolution of new and wholesome mental life, was for me a damning influence. Religion

> might have saved me, for I was one of those beings to whom
> hereditary potencies had made religion a necessary buoy and
> guide. Convinced that all such faith was foundationless and vain,
> I saw in life merely a farce, and chose to play my part there with
> an equal contempt for the performance itself and the fellow actors
> among whom I strutted my little hour.[12]

Such soliloquies as this recur throughout the manuscript, as Mountstuart
constructs the logic which makes him into a *new* Nero—not merely one among a
crowd of individuals who, throughout history, have perpetrated atrocities, but a
genuine innovation. In an age dominated by faith, as he observes, his lack of feeling
would not have been a problem, because external constraints on his behavior
would have made that defect irrelevant. Once rationalism and atheism became
available to him, however, the hereditary fault which made him incapable of love
and sympathy had to prove fatal to his personal morality.

Even Fanshawe realizes this in the end. After Theobald's revelation concerning
the true authorship of the manuscript, the doctor suggests that Fanshawe
should become Lancewood's literary executor. Fanshawe is quick to observe that
the manuscript ought to be published: "It's very horrible; but it's not a mere ghost-
liness and boogabooism. There's a meaning behind it." When Theobald asks him
to clarify, he goes on: "The bitter and terrible one that all great popular spiritual
and intellectual advancement necessitates ruin and death to a certain minority.
Harold Mountstuart is a voice that speaks for the minority, and with language of
mighty despair!"[13]

Although Mountstuart uses his private laboratory for nothing more exotic
than cooking up poisons, he is—like Douglas Duane and Kenneth Stafford—one of
the casualties of progress. Fawcett, in fact, shows us only the casualties; he
never—in spite of his championship of progress—shows us its beneficiaries.

The frame-narrative enclosing the story of *The Ghost of Guy Thyrle* concerns
a rather highly-strung student named Raymond Savernay, who has come down
from Oxford to spend the summer with his married brother Cecil. While at Oxford
he has become fascinated by the work of the Society for Psychical Research and the
possibility of finding rational explanatory accounts for "psychic phenomena." In
pursuit of this interest he visits a house owned by Cecil, and which is supposed to
be haunted by the ghost of one Guy Thyrle. At first he fails to see anything odd,
but returning one day to recover an ornamental matchbox left in the house, he finds
himself confronted by the nebulous specter of a young man.

Raymond now follows Cecil to London to tell him the whole story which
the ghost imparts to him, and Cecil in his turn relays the tale to the family doctor.
Cecil is panic-stricken because Raymond has said that the ghost is condemned to a
terrible fate from which it can only be released through the voluntary self-sacrifice
of another human being, and Cecil fears that this terrible delusion may be the prelude to a suicide attempt.

When it comes to be time for the reader to be told the story of Guy Thyrle,
Fawcett is cautious about how it is to be told, and the auctorial voice of the frame-
narrative observes that:

> The story was given [by Cecil to Dr. Leverett] in a far more
> broken and hesitant way than when he had heard it from Ray-
> mond's lips. At times, too, he even stumbled or halted outright in
> the telling of it. What he said will therefore not be recorded in his

own language. It has indeed been thought best to borrow neither his nor the more convincing voice of his brother, but to unfold in coming pages an impersonal chronicle, as though rearranged by one closely aware of all the leading facts, mindful that each of these shall secure due saliency of presentation, and conscientious in retaining whatever drama, poetry, or spiritual suggestion the original record may have disclosed."[14]

The inevitable result of this strategy is to imply that the story of Guy Thyrle is to be taken literally—like the story told in *A Romance of Two Brothers*—but Fawcett had already declared adamantly in the proem that "If certain readers choose to decide that Guy Thyrle's weird experiences wore other than the coinage of Raymond Savernay's hallucination, it is not because I have failed to give them full liberty to form an opposite belief." This is, of course, further testimony to the difficulty Fawcett had in maintaining the ambiguity of his story, and to the conviction of necessity which led him to do so.

Thyrle's story is by now a familiar one. He begins life as a lonely and introverted child, but when he eventually goes to Cambridge he proves to be brilliant in the field of chemistry. He is not popular with his peers, but forms a friendship with Vincent Ardilange. Ardilange is merely using Thyrle because he knows that the latter's income will set them both up in a house in London, whereas his own means are inadequate to secure this end. Thyrle does not suspect Ardilange of hypocrisy, though, and is glad to provide the financial backing for his friend's forays into London society.

Thyrle secludes himself in his laboratory, working upon the isolation of a drug named Onarline. He expects its effects to be psychotropic and probably hallucinogenic, but finds instead that it liberates the mind from the body, allowing the *persona* to roam where it will while the body lies inert, as if dead. With the laboratory work complete he decides to take time off to consider the implications of his discovery, and begins to accompany Ardilange on his social excursions. Ardilange resents what he sees as an intrusion, but can hardly object. His resentment grows when many of his acquaintances take more readily to Thyrle than to him, and he becomes passionately jealous when a girl he admires, Violet Fythian, becomes enamored of Thyrle. Thyrle also falls in love with her.

Thyrle tests his drug by locking himself in a hotel room and wandering about London in an invisible and incorporeal form. Matter is no barrier to him, and he learns that by an effort of will he can read the "psychic spectra" of others, obtaining insight into their moral character. Unfortunately, his inert body is discovered by a chambermaid, and he is only just in time to reclaim it before he is declared dead. As a precaution against similar problems, he takes Ardilange into his confidence and asks him to stand guard over the deserted body during the next experiment. Ardilange is at this time the benefactor of Thyrle's will, though this situation will inevitably change when Thyrle marries Violet, and Ardilange is so embittered against his friend that the opportunity to benefit from an undetectable murder is too good to miss.

Thyrle widens the scope of his researches to examine the whole state of human civilization. His second odyssey takes him all over the world. He examines the secret dealings of emperors and the squalid circumstances of their subjects. He sees human suffering and misery on a terrible scale, but finds hope for the future in the developing tendencies of altruism and charity—a moral evolution which seems to point the way to salvation. He visits the bowels of the Earth, tracking the fossil record within the rocks that tells the story of the evolution of life and of mankind.

He visits the ocean depths, and then soars outward into space. He finds the moon to be a long-dead world that was once Earth-like, and he explores the ruins of its extinct civilization. When he returns to Earth, however, he finds that he has been betrayed. Ardilange has had him declared dead, and his body has been cremated. His spirit is homeless.

Thyrle finds himself quite alone; though he has proved that the spirit exists independently of the body, and is at least potentially immortal, he can find no other spirits. They, it is clear, have some other destiny to which they may proceed, and are not confined as he is to the material cosmos. He sets off on a journey across the universe, determined to seek out this further world, craving an interview with God. God proves to be inaccessible, but Thyrle eventually manages to establish communication—albeit of a rather enigmatic character—with other beings of pure spirit.

They tell him that he may cross the threshold into the world beyond only if he can persuade another human being to surrender his life and allow Thyrle's spirit to share the moment of his death. He returns to Earth and finds that he can, under exceptional circumstances, make himself manifest to the living. Alas, such manifestations cause extreme alarm, and when he appears to Violet Fythian—immediately before her marriage to Ardilange—the shock kills her. He is extremely upset by this, and he takes his revenge for all the evil done to him by appearing to Ardilange and prompting his suicide. This done, he waits patiently with the hope that his strange imprisonment may one day end—as, indeed, it does when he convinces Raymond Savernay of the truth of his story. Cecil and the doctor are, of course, too late to save Raymond: they find him dying, and the last words uttered by his lips purport to come from the soul of Guy Thyrle.

Such is the plot of Fawcett's last realistic romance. It is not particularly convincing, and *as a plot* represents little advance over *Douglas Duane*. What sets the work in an entirely different class, however, is the fact that for the first time Fawcett really took advantage of the possibilities opened up by his hypothesis. Thyrle's revenge on Ardilange is really a matter of very little significance within the book by comparison with the wonders which the disembodied spirit beholds as it journeys across the universe. It presents not only an overview of the empire of man, but a vision of the whole of creation.

In all his previous realistic romances Fawcett had been concerned with individuals. The discoveries made in the stories are evaluated in terms of the effects which they have on their makers and others intimately connected with their makers. The great issues of the war between scepticism and belief are examined in terms of their effect on the psychology of individuals. Such consequences as there might be within the ideas raised by the stories for mankind as a whole are barely touched, even in Douglas Duane's moment of total revelation. Guy Thyrle's ghost sees less than Duane, and his experience has not the same quality of revelatory omniscience, but there is some *detail* in what he sees, and thus there is considerable substance in what he has to tell us about the greater world beyond our limited horizons of perception. It is this substance which was conspicuously lacking in Douglas Duane's account of what befell him in the wilderness of infinity.

Thyrle's journey has several distinct stages, each one offering a new expansion of perspective. It thus bears a structural similarity to the two most important cosmic voyage stories of the nineteenth and twentieth centuries: Camille Flammarion's *Lumen* and Olaf Stapledon's *Star Maker*. The first phase of his adventure allows him to survey the human world from the standpoint of a new objectivity. He can eavesdrop on world leaders and count the full cost of human misery, and can offer summary opinion on the entire human condition:

In this squalor, breeding pestilence as it does, I behold the soil from which that baleful flower of Anarchy has bloomed. Every red petal of it means the blood of countless accursed lives. Cholera itself, and all scourges like it, are indeed a sort of anarchy. Surely there must be some answer to this awful inequality between the rich and poor. Massacre and rapine are but a ridiculous answer. The men who dream that they can better the world by killing kings forget that they merely fortify with martyrs the cause they would crush. The men who dream of great co-operative commonwealths forget that in thousands of their own race lie greeds, egotisms, and evil passions, which would soon make life for the masses more burdensome still... The only hope, through millions of coming years, is in science. Some mighty force may be discovered amid the unexplored mysteries of Nature that will enable mankind to live without labour—as, for example, the wondrous turning of the common, inexhaustible air into food and raiment. If there be another hope, its name is fraternity, human love. Not merely the love that gives, but the love that abdicates and renounces.[15]

The second stage of the journey, into the rocks of the Earth's crust and the ocean depths, sets mankind into an environmental and evolutionary context. The third, which takes him to the moon, offers him a glimpse of a standard by which human civilization might be judged—an echo of a lunar culture which passed through the stage which human history has reached to achieve a kind of Utopia. (It is significant that this lunar race is now long-extinct, for the calm acceptance of their own mortality is one of the key elements of their maturity.)

The fourth stage of the journey sets the world of man in its cosmic context; in the space of a few pages it attempts to convey something of the awesome diversity of the universe and its millions of inhabited worlds. He finds many worlds where life has never developed, and many where it has perished. He finds, too, that the "men" of other worlds are frequently unhuman in form, intelligent life having many different ancestors. He describes people descended from Lizards and Lions whose cultural achievements are superior to man's, "splendid winged beings," giants and pygmies, and people intoxicated by the love of death. All the time, his perceptions are accelerating:

He swept onwards, past systems and systems of unrecorded stars. Here it was the same as among those astral cohorts which the sky-gazers of earth had science visually to observe and count. Suns, moons, planets, asteroids, in numbers incalculable! Worlds that yet were floating coils and wreaths and ragged drifts of vapour; worlds that yet were prodigious heavenly bonfires, fed by showers of attracted meteors and even by occasional vast nomadic comets; worlds that teemed with a beauty eclipsing the conception of man; worlds hideous beyond all human belief; worlds just born, youthful, matured, dying, or dead; worlds of sin, degradation and debauchery; worlds of chastity, idealism and peace; worlds in which not a single animal or vegetable shape bore the faintest likeness to those we meet on earth; worlds in which trees thought and spoke and saw; worlds that were earth in miniature or a thousand-fold magnified; worlds in which wolves, serpents, tigers, birds, and countless other creatures of indescribable sort, had won mastery, and risen by inflexible laws of evolution to that same superiority over their primary conditions which marks the ascendancy of earthly man over his ancestral ape.[16]

This passage then becomes the prelude to the final phase of the journey, wherein Thyrle attempts to transcend the material universe altogether, to enter the world of spirits and hold conversation with God. In this project he attains only incomplete success, but he does indeed obtain some testimony as to the nature and concerns of God.

This unfolding cosmic vision is extremely crude by comparison with Stapledon's *Star Maker*—only partly by necessity. Nevertheless, it is an achievement to be applauded. Most earlier accounts of the cosmos had been written from a religious standpoint; perhaps the most famous cosmic voyage previously undertaken was that of Emmanuel Swedenborg, who gave his own account of life on many worlds in one section of the *Arcana Coelestia*. Whether Fawcett knew of this work, or of any of its imitations, is not clear. There is a stronger likelihood that he had seen the early version of Flammarion's *Lumen* that was published in *Stories of Infinity*: there are several points of similarity between Thyrle's account of life on other worlds and Flammarion's. These might easily be coincidental, even when one counts in the more fragile echoes to be found in *Douglas Duane*, but a much closer parallel can be found between one of the other *Stories of Infinity*, "History of a Comet," and a poem by Fawcett called "The Comet" which was published in *Fantasy and Passion*.

Even if Fawcett *had* read *Lumen*, however, there is a greater significance in the differences between Lumen's voyage and Guy Thyrle's than in the similarities. *Lumen* is an imaginative *tour de force* of great power, but it sits squarely astride the gulf between the religious imagination and the scientific imagination: it is the ultimate fantasy of spiritualism, in which the revelations of science and the primary dogmas of religious faith are harmonized into a peculiar syncretic amalgam. We have already seen that Fawcett was attracted by such a prospect, and how he attempted a similar binding in *Douglas Duane*. In *The Ghost of Guy Thyrle*, however—despite the invocation of the Society for Psychical Research in the frame narrative and the frank acceptance both of the existence of God and the immortality of the soul, Fawcett is content to set the material and spiritual worlds apart. God's relationship with his creation here is much less intimate than the spiritualists wanted to believe. The ghost of Guy Thyrle is real enough, but a corollary of its explanation is that *there are no others*. Thyrle exists, for a brief span of time, in an intermediate dimension between the material and the spiritual, but once his situation is resolved, the link is broken. Fawcett will have none of the notion of serial reincarnation that was so vital to Flammarion's image of the cosmic scheme—it is entirely alien to his viewpoint. Fawcett's God resembles the gods of the early Greek atomists, who may or may not exist but are in any case remote from their creation and uninvolved with it, leaving the material world to be understood in its own terms, by reference to its own principles of construction and regulation. Despite its glimpses of the nature of deity, *The Ghost of Guy Thyrle* is a thoroughly agnostic work. In this respect it looks forward to *Star Maker* rather than backward to *Lumen*.

There is easily enough that is of interest in Fawcett's realistic romances to establish him as an important figure in the "prehistory" of science fiction. He demands attention from the archaeologist of the imagination, if from no one else. His long-time absence from historical studies of the genre is puzzling, but this injustice is being slowly set to rights. *The Ghost of Guy Thyrle* is annotated in the Salem Press *Survey of Science Fiction Literature*, while that work and *Solarion* are both annotated in the second edition of *Anatomy of Wonder*.

In conclusion, however, it is perhaps appropriate to set aside questions of Fawcett's relevance within the history of literary traditions, and to look instead at one or two unique features of his work in terms of their psychological significance. The most one can hope to derive from such an exercise is an account of certain personal idiosyncrasies, but it is worth noting that even a man's personal idiosyncrasies may be the products of the time in which he lives.

The most striking feature characteristic of Fawcett's realistic romances is his insistence on retaining the ambiguity of the main narrative. One might be tempted to regard this simply as an insurance against implausibility, but in certain instances Fawcett's attempts to sustain the ambiguity itself becomes implausible. Admirers of the structuralist Tzvetan Todorov might interpret this differently; for Todorov the definitive characteristic of "the fantastic" as opposed to "the marvellous" is precisely this kind of ambiguity, and he would presumably see Fawcett's overemphasis on ambiguity as an essential corollary of his declared intention to characterize with his writings a new genre.

In fact, it seems more likely that the determination of the author to make his speculative fictions ambiguous is a corollary of his committed agnosticism. The realistic romances deal, *by definition*, with the unknowable, and it is essential according to Fawcett's positivistic way of thinking that the unknowable cannot be made known. It therefore has to be handled in a very special way: the speculative element in fantastic fiction must somehow be distanced from the reader so that it makes no direct claim upon his beliefs in the way that a mundane fictional narrative is entitled to do.

Outside of this technical concern, however, one cannot help feeling that the determined ambiguity of the realistic romances—and, indeed, Fawcett's agnosticism itself—overlies a deep-seated ambivalence in his own attitude. While feeling that reason forced him to reject such ideas as the immortality of the soul, Fawcett seems to have felt their loss very deeply indeed. Though his own commited faith forbade him ever to recapture a naive belief in the certainty of an afterlife, the notion itself continued to attract his attention and to draw heavily upon the resources of his imagination.

The protagonists of Fawcett's realistic romances are always more extreme in their beliefs than he was. They become too easily cold and derelict of feeling; lack of religious faith tempts them frequently towards lack of conscience. The stories in which they suffer, sometimes terribly, in consequence of their own brilliance, are stories of awful warning and promises of punishment for careless sin. Fawcett presumably never felt himself guilty of the sins which these characters commit, but his preoccupation with them nevertheless suggests a sense of personal hazard.

It seems probable that Edgar Fawcett's agnosticism was hard-won, and that while he maintained it staunchly, he was well aware of its costs. He regarded his own views as a necessary advancement of human knowledge and intelligence; as a gain in evolutionary *fitness* (for Spencer, who coined the phrase, "the survival of the fittest" meant the survival of the most intellectually advanced). In his romantic fiction, however, it was Fawcett's fears rather than his hopes which rose to the surface; the pessimistic spirit of Schopenhauer proved more demanding of his inspiration than the optimism of Spencer. This should not surprise us; anyone familiar with the history of imaginative fiction will know that it has very often been the case.

ALGEBRAIC FANTASIES & REALISTIC ROMANCES, by Brian Stableford

AUTHOR'S NOTE

I am greatly indebted to the Alderman Library of the University of Virginia, whose staff supplied microfilm copies of *A Romance of Two Brothers* and *The New Nero*, and a photocopy of the relevant pages of *Songs of Doubt and Dream*.

IV.

THE POLITICS OF EVOLUTION

PHILOSOPHICAL THEMES IN THE
SPECULATIVE FICTION OF M. P. SHIEL

There is a certain hazard in examining the work of any novelist in search of "philosophical themes." Students of an author's work are frequently warned that it may be a terrible mistake to infer the beliefs and opinions of an author from the ideas possessed and expressed by his characters. The hazard is real enough, in that a man might write about perverse theologians, moral derelicts, and political fanatics without being any of these things himself.

It is with especial caution that one must approach the work of a writer like M. P. Shiel, because he was a writer who deliberately dealt with bizarre characters and peculiar situations, and who took a delight in startling his readers with unusual moral judgments and evaluations. It is, in a way, rather remarkable that in addition to all this he clearly did use his fiction—especially his speculative fiction—as a means of preaching his own idiosyncratic creeds. Many of the arguments deployed by characters in his stories can be found in much the same form in the posthumous collection of Shiel's essays edited by John Gawsworth, *Science, Life and Literature*.

Science, Life and Literature provides a good guide to the business of sorting out which of the ideas expressed by Shiel's characters are really his own. The question then arises, however, as to why, if Shiel's ideas are available in "pure" non-fictional form, one needs to analyze his fiction in order to rediscover them. An examination of the fiction allows us to see something of the growth and development of Shiel's theories as well as their conclusive form, but a much more important reason is the manner in which Shiel's fiction displays and exemplifies his philosophy in a way that essays never could. The fiction shows the implications of his patterns of thought for the way that men ought to behave and evaluate the actions of others. The behavior of Shiel's characters very often seems peculiar, and an understanding of the underlying context of thought can provide a necessary illumination of the logic of their behavior. Conversely, the ideas themselves are dramatized and clarified by an examination of their expressions in this way.

Shiel was a writer rather prone to lecturing his readers, or letting his characters do it for him. Often this material seems to be entirely extraneous to the plot, as when Caxton Hazlitt summarizes Shiel's firmest convictions in his conversations with Mahndorla in *How the Old Woman Got Home* (1927). Even here the intrusion is less arbitrary than it seems, but in general his dramas of contemporary life are less revealing of the Shielian philosophy than his speculative fiction. When he writes of the future, or of fantastic experiments in the present, his philosophy becomes the very foundation-stone of his imaginary endeavor. This essay, in consequence, will concentrate mainly on analysis of Shiel's seven major scientific romances.

If the foregoing argument needs re-emphasis, it can be obtained from an inspection of one of Shiel's most substantial essays, "On Writing," which is derived—along with its companion-piece "On Reading"—from an open letter used as a preface to *This Knot of Life* (1909). Here, Shiel's view on the nature of art not only encourages us to read his work with an eye to its underlying philosophy, but virtually demands that we should do so. He begins by likening the writer to a messenger-boy, and suggests that excellence in writing is no more than excellence in delivering a message. The message, he concedes, should be decently clothed, but it is the requirements of the *matter* to be conveyed by the message that are most important:

> And as to his matter, we can at once say what it must be: it must be a true message; and then it must be a new message—fresh news; and then it must somehow be a message about yourself, of some interest to *you*; or, bracketing all this into an abstract form—he must *enlarge your consciousness of the truth of things*, and that intimately.
> This, then, as to matter, is your task.
> And if you ask, "But is the object of Art precisely the object of science and of philosophy—to enlarge the consciousness?" the reply is, "Yes—what else than to enlarge the consciousness," i.e., to augment the quantity of Life, i.e., to cause Progress in Life—"that we may have Life, and have it more abundantly?" Nevertheless, the method of Art, though more after the method of philosophy, is as divided from it as the method of philosophy from that of science. Art, for instance, is more intimate and about ourselves somehow, enlarging our consciousness of the truth of our own hearts, and bosoms' biology principally, and affecting us in an intimate way by a particular kind of tickling of one or other of the five senses. Besides, though the object of Art, like that of philosophy, is the demonstration of some abstract fact, Art does not, as philosophy does, formally state this, but conveys it intimately, as by innuendo and parable, in a glance, a sob, ineffably, in the tone of gossips pottering over a dead body; and it is divided from science, and from philosophy also, in this, that even the facts that it formally states are not concrete, but are themselves, like its abstract facts, abstractions: for, if it tells of a man, an axe, it is not any actual man or axe that exists exactly as it tells of it, as in Dickens, but it is an abstraction from a mass of actual men or axes of that class, like Hamlet, or Hector's axe, or Gainsborough's *Grace*. And so we get clearly the difference between science, philosophy and art.[1]

This quotation provides us with adequate grounds not only for the view that the messages embedded in Shiel's fiction are to be taken seriously, but also for the view that consideration of the ideas in their fictional form will reveal a special dimension within them.

It should, perhaps, be added that there are several reasons why this project may be of interest to students of speculative fiction. For one thing, much critical writing about Shiel has neglected analysis of his themes in favor of comment upon his unorthodox and sometimes colorful literary style. More importantly, Shiel's underlying philosophy has been widely misrepresented by commentators. Even his most ardent champion, A. Reynolds Morse, sometimes gives a misleading impression of Shiel's work and its purpose, while comments on Shiel by Sam Moskowitz are decidedly unwarranted. Then too, the themes themselves are of some interest—not (as Shiel would have hoped) because they constitute a significant contribution to modern thought, but because they represent an intriguing and idiosyncratic product of their particular period and intellectual climate.

M. P. Shiel was born in the West Indies in 1865. He was the son of a Methodist preacher, but records in an autobiographical sketch that between the ages of 11 and 14 he turned against the faith of his father. (Conversion to freethought by the sons of clergymen is curiously common among the early writers of scientific romance; George Griffith, William Hope Hodgson and John Beresford did likewise. The zeal which converts of any kind characteristically devote to self-justification may have been an element in leading these writers to dabble in scientifically-based speculative fantasy.)

In his later teens Shiel was sent to King's College, London. He then taught for a while before attending Bart's Hospital for some months with the intention of becoming a doctor. He drifted instead into the literary world, though little is known of how he occupied his time until he began to write for the popular magazines that were proliferating in the 1890s. His first book, *Prince Zaleski,* was published in 1895. This collection and *Shapes in the Fire* (1895) were issued by John Lane, and were contemporary with Lane's *Yellow Book.* Both volumes share with the work most typical of the *Yellow Book* a self-conscious decadence and an interest in unconventional philosophies of art and life. These affectations are superimposed on stories which are apparently inspired by Poe: Dupinesque detective stories in the first volume, horror stories in the second.

Shiel remained a prolific writer almost until the outbreak of World War I. As well as sixteen novels and three collections for which he was solely responsible, he wrote numerous works in collaboration with Louis Tracy (usually in the way of helping Tracy out with his hack-writing commitments when time was pressing), and one short novel in collaboration with the famous journalist, W. T. Stead (this collaboration consisted of Shiel's writing down a story told to him verbally by Stead). Between 1914 and 1922, however, Shiel published nothing. In his sketch "About Myself," he does not account for this nine-year gap but simply passes over it in silence. He published one novel in 1923, but did not begin to produce work on a regular basis again until 1927. Six more novels and two collections appeared between then and 1937, plus a series of reprints from the early part of his career in which the texts were sometimes heavily revised. In the last decade of his life he published nothing more, though he left one unpublished novel, *The Splendid Devil,* and had been working for some years on a novelization of the career of Jesus. He died in 1947.

Shiel was an idiosyncratic author who was happy in his defiance of any kind of categorization. His prose is fluent, and displays an unusual vocabulary in characteristically flamboyant fashion. Although colorful, his style is not highly adjectival (in "On Writing" he comments that "Writers, and... minds of any strength in general, cherish a natural dislike for adjectives"), and even his most exotic passages are unlike commonly-encountered purple prose. His syntax is often eccentric and his punctuation luxuriant, but he had a careful regard for the actual rules of grammar, if not its customs, and he always paid attention to the rhythmic qualities of his prose. He occasionally pressed his idiosyncrasies to wild excess, especially in his earliest work—they are at their most amazing in *Shapes in the Fire*—but for the most part he remains an eminently readable writer, though perhaps something of an acquired taste. When his subject matter is mundane the floridity of his writing—especially where it extends to the dialogue—frequently seems bizarre, but when his themes are fantastic enough the style can seem perfectly adapted, as in *The Purple Cloud* (1901), the brilliant short story, "Dark Lot of One Saul" (in *Here Comes the Lady*, 1928), and the alien encounter sequence of *The Young Men Are Coming* (1937).

One thing that must always be remembered in analyzing Shiel's work, especially in respect of the early stories, is that he clearly took a delight in startling his readers. His plots and commentaries are very often shaped in order to shock, and to defy the expectations of the reader. He loved to strike a pose at once casual and provocative, to give offense in a carefree, but never unsubtle, fashion. This is obvious enough in his long "philosophical essays," including "Premier and Maker" in *Shapes in the Fire* and Cummings King Monk's definition of Greatness of Mind in *The Pale Ape* (1911).

This is not to say that Shiel's opinions were not sincerely held, but simply that the *outré* and the unpopular had a natural attraction for him. He was one of those thinking men who would avoid orthodoxy at any price, and was sufficiently adept in the art of rhetoric to convince himself fairly easily that the orthodox opinion in any matter was not only obviously wrong but contemptible. He carved out his own intellectual and artistic niche, and cared far more about being a writer *sui generis* than courting popularity or making money. In his comments on other writers he was determinedly iconoclastic, and particularly so when dealing with writers who might be perceived as having something in common with himself. H .G. Wells, who was also interested in the evolutionary progress of man, the advancement of science, and the cause of socialism, is several times slighted in *Science, Life and Literature*, particularly in the essay "Of Writing and Science," which casts aside the entire *genre* of scientific romance as unworthy of serious consideration. There was, however, no personal hostility between the two men, who exchanged letters on friendly terms.

Shiel is accused by his critics of many sins: of anticlericalism, of overt racism, of antisemitism, of incipient Nazism, of social Darwinism, and of commitment to the morality of negative eugenics. Some of these accusations he might have welcomed, most he would have dismissed as crass errors. His actual intellectual position was much more complicated than any of these labels can imply, and none of his opinions was held unthinkingly. One can see how unsympathetic readers might easily become infuriated by him, but he cannot be casually dismissed by association with exploded dogmas: he had his own reasons for saying what he had to say.

Shiel's early novels were mostly written as serials for the popular magazines, and tend to be colorful adventure stories packed with action. The first of them was serialized in *Short Stories* as "The Empress of the Earth," and reprinted in book form as *The Yellow Danger* in 1898. The story was apparently written at the suggestion of Louis Tracy, who was one of several writers of the period to make his name writing future war stories. Tracy's own reputation was largely based on *The Final War* (1896), which had been serialized in another magazine run by C. Arthur Pearson, the publisher of *Short Stories*. Both Tracy's novel and Shiel's were steeped in the mythology of a "war to end war," though the two writers characterized this climax in human affairs in very different ways.

The Yellow Danger is the story of a crucial confrontation between East and West—between the yellow race and the white—to settle the permanent dominion of the world. A personal element is introduced into the plot on the one hand by virtue of the fact that the evil genius directing the Oriental forces, Dr. Yen How, is romantically obsessed with an English girl named Ada Seward, and on the other hand by the heroic efforts of an English midshipman, John Hardy, whose enterprise thwarts Yen How's master plan.

The plot is as unsubtle as it is unlikely. The invasion of the Western World is effected by the simple but implausible ploy of having the entire population of China walk steadily westwards, while military support is given mainly (and ineptly) by the Japanese navy. In the end, the fleet which set forth for England, following the sinking of the warships, is towed northwards and fed to the Maelstrom. A handful of prisoners is then infected with a deadly plague and released in mainland Europe in order to wipe out the massed hordes of the East encamped there. It is a rather nasty-minded novel, and has the dubious distinction of having introduced the mythology of the "yellow peril" to English popular fiction. Shiel went on to write other novels of a not-dissimilar kind, though *The Yellow Wave* (1905) is not really a yellow peril story and features a very different resolution to the war to end war, and *The Dragon* (1913; reprinted in 1929 as *The Yellow Peril*) is very much more subtle in conception and execution than *The Yellow Danger*. The man who really milked the idea for all it was worth was, of course, Sax Rohmer (Arthur S. Ward), who invented the insidious Dr. Fu Manchu.

Most of the future-war novels which were produced so prolifically between 1871 and 1914 involved conflicts restricted to Europe. Nation-states were the contending parties. Tracy's *Final War,* though it is mainly concerned with a secret alliance of France, Germany, and Russia intended to smash the British Empire, actually broke with tradition in introducing a fierce note of racial chauvinism. The last chapter of that novel is given over to an essay in frenzied rhetoric where England's victory against her enemies is held to be the culmination of the destiny of the Anglo-Saxon race. The destiny of the other races is to submit to the enlightened rule of this chosen people.

Shiel in The *Yellow Danger seems* to be taking up this theme. The ideative framework of the novel is established very early in the text as a quasi-Darwinistic struggle for existence between the two leading contenders for dominion. Yen How, discussing the future with a Japanese statesman, paints the following picture:

> "Look forward five hundred, a thousand years, Marquis, and what do you see?" answered Yen How. "Is it not this?—the white man and the yellow man in their death-grip, contending for the earth. The white and the yellow—there are no others. The black is the slave of both; the brown does not count. But there are those two; and when the day comes that they stand face to face in dreadful hate, saying, 'One or other must quit this earth,' shall I tell you which side will win?"
> "Which do you think?"
> "The white will win, Marquis."[2]

Yen How goes on to argue that the white race has already advanced further along the path of progress, and that because progress is exponential, will draw further ahead with every generation that passes. His attempt to overwhelm the West is by way of being a pre-emptive strike against the odds. Given the social-Darwinist framework, the fact that the war ends with a virtual genocide is not entirely surprising.

In terms of Shiel's development, *The Yellow Danger* is most important as a reservoir of ideas which he later abandoned or modified considerably. It is in every sense a naive book. (Shiel did prepare a revised edition for possible publication in the thirties under the title *China in Arms*, but it was universally rejected as too dated.) Shiel did not entirely abandon social Darwinism, and he maintained the notion that the men of the West were in general more "highly evolved" than colored men, but he ceased thinking in the crude terms which dominate The *Yellow Danger*, largely because his notion of evolution became much more sophisticated—he adopted, in fact, a distinctly un-Darwinian philosophy of evolution which derived mainly from Herbert Spencer. He became more interested in the cultural aspects of the differences between nations and ceased to regard them as quasi-Darwinian subspecies necessarily locked in a winner-take-all struggle for existence.

Attention should, however, be drawn to one aspect of *The Yellow Danger* which seems rather arbitrary, but which is characteristic of Shiel: before all issues are finally settled he kills off his hero in an utterly pointless duel. Within the sole context of the novel, this seems to be no more than a callous flourish—perhaps a simple refusal to bow to convention—but in the context of the whole canon it assumes a greater, if enigmatic, significance. There can be few writers who have ever treated their heroes with such a marked lack of generosity as Shiel. It is not simply that they often die, or that their cherished projects frequently fail—they are often made to be victims of their own stupidity, moving uncertainly from one awkward situation to another. They *are* heroes, but always flawed, and they receive no concessions from fate (as managed by the author) on account of their heroic status. In any individual book this tends to seem merely whimsical, but the pattern is not without its rationale, and in fact testifies to a fundamental aspect of Shiel's worldview.

After three mundane adventure novels, Shiel returned to futuristic romance with a plan for an ambitious three-volume project, the various parts of which were subsequently detached from one another and presented as unlinked works. Indeed, they never at any time constituted a trilogy in the usual sense of the word, the connection between them being peculiar and rather tenuous.

The introduction to the first of these three works, *The Lord of the Sea* (dropped from the revised version published in 1929), represents the main narrative as having been transcribed from statements made by a medium in trance. The medium, Mary Wilson, is said in this introduction to have had many more-or-less coherent visions of the future, but only four notebooks are forwarded by her doctor to the hypothetical author for publication. *The Lord of the Sea* is said to be notebook II in the series, and the hypothetical author expresses his intention of publishing books I and III as *The Last Miracle* and *The Purple Cloud*. The book versions of *The Lord of the Sea* and *The Purple Cloud* were, in fact, published in the same year (1901), but *The Last Miracle* did not follow until 1906. Although the introduction does not say so, the visions are apparently of alternative futures; despite one or two trivial background links, the three stories cannot be fitted into a single future-historical framework.

It is *The Lord of the Sea* which has occasioned the fiercest attack mounted on Shiel, by Sam Moskowitz in his collection of essays, *Explorers of the Infinite*. Moskowitz alleges that:

> *The Lord of the Sea* reaches an intensity of anti-Semitism that provokes comparison with Hitler's *Mein Kampf*, for which it could have served as an inspiration.[3]

After his summary of the novel, which does little justice to the complexity of the plot or the scope of its ideas, Moskowitz adds:

Only in his prediction that Palestine would flourish under the Jews does Shiel's novel show any merit, either in prophecy, prose or decency. It need scarcely be emphasized that the only difference between his method and the Nazis' rests in the fact that he would have permitted the Jews to emigrate with their lives.[4]

Other readers have wondered how Moskowitz came to this conclusion, and have commented on its strangeness (James Blish and Dale Mullen have both taken the trouble to criticize the view in print). There is a certain amount of anti-semitic comment in the book, and its villain, Frankl, is characterized rather after the fashion of Shylock and Fagin as a stereotyped grasping Jew of the kind that one finds in very many British works of the late nineteenth and early twentieth centuries. Considered in the context of the literature of the time, this would be unpleasant but by no means unusual; but what is more important is that the rest of the material in *The Lord of the Sea,* insofar as it relates to Jews individually or collectively, is far from anti-semitic. The hero of the book is also a Jew (indeed, he is the Messiah who returns the Jews to the promised land—he issues an edict banishing all the Jews to Palestine, but does so in order that a prophecy shall be fulfilled, not because he hates them).

At the beginning of The *Lord of the Sea* the nations of continental Europe pass edicts expelling Jews from their territory. England becomes their haven, and the influx of Jewish refugees brings "a tide of prosperity... as has hardly been known in a country." The Jews become a powerful political and economic force, but their influence seems almost entirely benign. An exception to this rule, however, is Baruch Frankl, who acquires a country estate and (for reasons not altogether clear) orders his tenants to adopt the fez as a symbol of their servitude. This imposition causes great resentment and precipitates a feud between the landlord and a young farmer named Richard Hogarth. The feud is complicated by the fact that Frankl's daughter Rebekah is in love with Hogarth, while Frankl harbors lustful desires in respect of Hogarth's sister Margaret. Though Hogarth likes Rebekah, Margaret loathes Frankl.

Frankl eventually succeeds in having Hogarth framed for murder and has Margaret abducted into a lunatic asylum. Hogarth escapes from prison, taking along two other prisoners, and recovers from Frankl's estate a cache of meteoric diamonds with which he sets out to change the world. While in prison he has found what he believes to be an original plan for banishing social injustice from the world, and he intends to force the nations to adopt it. He claims territorial rights over the world's oceans, building gigantic floating fortresses to control the shipping lanes and enforce his title.

Hogarth's economic theory—which Shiel later claimed for his own—was actually not original, though the determined insistence on his independent discovery of it may imply that Shiel reached the conclusion on his own and only later discovered that he had been anticipated.

Hogarth's inspiration originates in the curious observation that a fisherman needs only to labor one day in six in order to catch enough to feed his family, whereas people working the land must make much more effort. As it is obvious to him that the land is more productive than the sea, it seems to him that the system of land-tenure must have something radically wrong with it. He decides that all land should be in common ownership, and that rents on land should be paid to the nation, thus providing the revenues which sustain the governmental and legal apparatus. Although not identical to it, this idea is very similar to the land tax system sketched out by the American socialist Henry George in his best-selling *Progress and Poverty* (1879). Like George, Hogarth has great faith in his single tax, and considers that the social consequences of its use would be good on humanitarian grounds, leading to a more egalitarian and less strife-ridden society.

Hogarth quickly establishes a stranglehold on world trade with the aid of his floating fortresses, and forces the nations to subscribe to a new manifesto embodying his theory of political economy.

The original version of the manifesto (*i.e.*, that given in the first edition of *The Lord of the Sea*) begins with a philosophical argument calculated to prove that a planet is "given" to its inhabitants, and that all people living on it should have an equal stake in it. Individuals who use various parcels of land for various purposes therefore should pay rent to mankind as a whole. The fact that groups of men claim dominion over particular areas of land (nations) is here seen as an iniquity, but Hogarth does not demand that the English quit England or the Chinese China—he merely demands that they should pay the rent on these countries to a World State. He applies the same argument to individuals within nations. The present state of the world is represented by Hogarth as a literal sin—an affront to divine law, but what he means by "divine law" is not quite what the Churchmen mean by it:

> But by far the greatest of the penalties which Nature has sent upon Man for this great violation is the arrest of Man's development. Man is a mind in an animal; the wing of mind is Pride, Assurance, or Self-esteem: and the home of an animal is a Planet. An animal without a home is (like curs and stray creatures) a thing without Assurance or Pride: so Man without the Earth is a mind without wing. So swift is he by nature, that, even so, he makes what we call 'progress': which is but crawling—now forward—now backward. This Progress, or Crawling, would assuredly become Flight, had his mind but its natural wing of Pride. But he lacks Assurance and foot-hold, firm home, and domain: though neither fish nor fowl, his sole heritage is sea, and air: the foxes have holes, and the birds of the air have nests, but the son of Man hath not where to lay his head: he is born into the home which God gave to his father, and finds it seized and sold.[5]

Here we see the beginning of a kind of deification of evolutionary progress. Despite his anti-Christianity, Shiel refused to proclaim himself an atheist or an agnostic (indeed, he denied the very possibility of atheism), but followed Thomas Henry Huxley in being prepared to be a deist only on the condition of a radical change in our concept of "God."

The second version of the manifesto differs from the first in detail but not in principle. The primacy of the World State is de-emphasized, the pattern of the argument running from individuals to nations to the world, rather than *vice versa*. The passage quoted above is modified very slightly, but in one respect significantly, so that under present conditions it is a favored few who, "having Assurance, make what we call 'Progress,' i.e., the discovering of truth—a crawling which might become flight, had all minds but the wing of Pride to co-operate in discovering truth."[6]

This is significant because of the emphasis on Progress as the result of a collective endeavor. Shiel believed firmly by 1929 that knowledge did *not* grow through the genius of the few, but through the seeking of the many. Individual discoveries he regarded as serendipitous rather than emblems of the mental superiority of their makers, and the number of discoveries made was, in his view, a mere statistical reflection of the number of people constructively active in the business of science.

In the novel, Hogarth's grand plan misfires. His empire collapses, but not because of any fault in his theory. The world, it is implied, *could* have been saved if the people had only listened—but the landlords and rich men would not. His attempt to impose reform by force could only succeed as long as he had the unswerving loyalty of the men aboard his fortresses, but Hogarth nestles a viper in his bosom in Patrick O'Hara, one of those who escaped prison with him. O'Hara destroys him, after a long sequence of petty betrayals which should have warned Hogarth not to trust him, but somehow does not.

The affair of transplanting the Jews to Palestine is one of the sub-plots of the story. In the early part of the story, Hogarth is enraged by Frankl into declaring that if he had the power he would send all the Jews back to Palestine. When he actually becomes Lord of the Sea, Hogarth is a very different man, and even Frankl as an individual becomes too small to hate. His angry outburst is quite forgotten, until Rebekah, inspired by prophecies uttered by a seeress, asks him to carry out his "threat" so that her people can fulfill their destiny. Hogarth agrees. At this point in time Hogarth does not know that he is a Jew himself, though his father once tried to tell him. Not until after his downfall does this fact become generally known, and Hogarth goes into exile too, where he is hailed by the Jews as the agent of their deliverance. He becomes their ruler, and in Palestine alone of all places on Earth his ideas are put into practice. Here, eventually, he sees the proof of his theory as the Promised Land does indeed flow with milk and honey and the most enthusiastic of Biblical prophecies are fulfilled:

> Here was not merely progress, but progress at increasing speed—acceleration—finally resembling flight, as of eagle or phoenix, eye fixed on the sun: Tyre by the fiftieth year having grown into the biggest of ports, her quays unloading 6,700,000 tons a year, mart of tangled masts, felucca, galiot, junk, cargoes of Tarshish and the Isles, Levantine stuffs, spice from the Southern Sea; while Jerusalem had grown into the recognized school of the wealthier youth of Europe, Asia and America.
>
> For it says: "The Kings of the earth shall bring their honour and glory unto her, and again, "She shall reign gloriously."
>
> And not Israel alone reaped the fruits of his own fine weather, but his dews fell wide. For it says: "They shall be as dew from the Lord"; and again: "They shall fill the face of the earth with fruit"; and again: "All nations shall call them blessed."
>
> And so it was: for the example of Israel, his suasive charm, proved compelling as sunshine to shoots, so that heart of Spinoza lived to see the spectacle of a whole world deserting the gory path of Rome to go up into those uplands of mildness and gleefulness whither invites the smile of that lily Galilean.
>
> The mission of "unbelieving" Israel was to convert Christendom to Christianity; and this he did.[7]

It hardly needs emphasizing that this is a most curious form of "antisemitism." This conclusion is, in part, a monumental literary flourish—a climax exotic enough to cap the many minor climaxes which fill the plot. Shiel did not believe that it was the Jews who would bring about a renewal of the real world, but he did believe, passionately, that such a renewal was possible and highly desirable.

Hogarth is perhaps the archetype of the Shielian flawed hero. He is brave and good and noble, and there is no doubting his intelligence or cleverness. And yet, still, he is something of a fool. The reader can only find it amazing that he fails to realize that O'Hara is a treacherous liar. While his mind is on great matters he is neglectful of his personal safety to a perilous degree, and is destroyed by his neglect. This pattern was to recur throughout Shiel's canon. Langler, in *The Last Miracle,* is incredibly stupid when he calmly tells the villain everything he knows about the latter's activities—an indiscretion which results in his sister's being mutilated. Llewellyn, in *This Knot of Life,* receives into his household a man who is his bitterest enemy, and permits that man to destroy his life. Cobby, in *Children of the Wind* (1923), fails to recognize his deadly enemy because of a shaven beard and false teeth—*despite the fact that the villain offers his own name.* Caxton Hazlitt, in *How the Old Woman Got Home,* is a very paradigm of stupidity, despite the fact that he is the mouthpiece for the fullest account of Shiel's opinions; his sins of omission and commission result in the death of his mother (whose welfare throughout is his main concern) and the ruination of an innocent girl. In part, the characters suffer from a kind of "negative paranoia" whereby they are incapable of suspecting that anyone is plotting against them even in the most obvious circumstances. They often show a related inability to bear grudges. It seems superficially ridiculous that these should be Shiel's "overmen"—his example to us all of what kind of men *should* live on earth but cannot because of the iniquities of our political institutions, but Shiel is both consistent and serious about this, and there is reason in it.

The Purple Cloud, which directly followed *The Lord of the Sea,* is rightly considered to be Shiel's most outstanding work. It is, in its way, a masterpiece. It is also a rather atypical book in Shiel's canon, insofar as one can speak of a "type" in respect of such a heterogenous *oeuvre.* Like *The Lord of the Sea* it is as much a theological fantasy as a scientific romance: it is an apocalyptic fantasy and the tale of a new Adam and Eve. It differs radically, as might be expected of Shiel, from other Adam and Eve stories, though it has noticeable affinities with the rash of "last man" fantasies which flourished briefly in the early part of the nineteenth century, including a novel by Mary Shelley and a long poem by Thomas Campbell.

Unlike The *Lord of the Sea* the story of *The Purple Cloud* appears to have been transmitted back to Mary Wilson by its hero (or perhaps, in this case, anti-hero might be a better description), for it is told as a first-person narrative. Its ostensible author begins by recalling the ranting of a Scottish preacher, who predicted that disaster would follow if any man reached the North Pole, because the pole is in some mysterious symbolic sense the Tree of the Knowledge of Good and Evil forbidden to man since the days of Adam.

In spite of this warning, the narrator—Adam Jeffson—is tempted by his fiancée to become part of an expedition to the pole. His place is won by murder, and a second murder is committed when Jeffson becomes incorporated into the small group making the Final dash for the pole. He thrusts on ahead of his companions and wins through to his goal, which he perceives as a pillar engraved with unreadable characters, surrounded by a lake of living fluid. This is an illusion, and he is plagued by hallucinations as he makes his way south again: the whole novel is a nightmare of guilt and encroaching madness and a transcendental voyage through an inner hell; this surreal experience in the Arctic is only the beginning.

Jeffson finds himself alone in a world from which all animal life has been exterminated by a poisonous purple gas released from a volcano. After searching for survivors and destroying London by fire, he begins to loot Europe for treasures which he intends to pile up in the richest palace the world has ever known, but he is periodically affected by bouts of despair that alternate with his waves of obsessive activity. (Many of Shiel's heroes are subject to bouts of deep gloom, and their activities frequently seem manic.)

The manuscript becomes fragmentary, breaking off at one point for a period of seventeen years, and seems quite surreal. Jeffson is tormented by opposing forces which seem to have used him throughout his life as their battleground. He characterizes them as "the white" and "the black" and considers himself the instrument of the latter, though the former will not let him go. At one point he finds in himself a symbol of the world, his moods and struggles reflecting the plight of the planet in its slow and fitful evolution.

Jeffson abandons himself to death on more than one occasion, but is preserved as if for some special purpose; but when he eventually finds the second survivor of the disaster—a girl, younger than the world's emptiness, born in an airtight chamber where her mother was imprisoned—he rebels against the plan by which "the white" seems intent on making him father to a new human race. He will not let the girl name herself Eve once she learns to speak, but instead names her after his murderous fiancée. She rejects that, and in the end they agree that she shall be named Leda.

Aware of the sufferings to which people were subject before the cloud, Jeffson is convinced that it is better that the race should not be re-created, but he knows that in this he is allying himself with the black. Leda's influence brings him only slowly back to sanity, and he resents the awful responsibility of it. He tries to abandon her and resolves to kill himself, but when she tells him over the telephone that she has again seen the purple cloud staining the horizon he gives way, and accepts that the human story must begin again. The fruit of the Tree of Knowledge of Good and Evil at last takes root inside him, and he accepts the law of God:

> For I, Adam Jeffson, parent of a race, hereby lay down, ordain, and decree for all time, perceiving it now: That the one motto and watchword proper to the riot and odyssey of Life in general, and in especial to the race of men, ever was, and remains, even this: "Though He slay me, yet I will trust in Him."[8]

Shiel was a great admirer of the Book of Job, naming its author as first among all writers for "Expression" and third (behind "the Jehovist" and Goethe) for "Matter." There is a good deal of Job in The *Purple Cloud,* which can be regarded, likewise, as an exploratory hypothesis explicating the relationship between human suffering (at the individual and total level) and the moral order of the universe. It is worth noting that Wells, too, wrote a new Book of Job in The *Undying Fire* (1919).

As in *The Lord of the Sea,* the theology of *The Purple Cloud* is odd, but orthodox in the sense that it takes its warrant from the Bible. If one reads the book in isolation it is not obvious that "the white" is a very different God from the God of the Churchmen. The dissolution of the idea of deity into the basic force animating the universe—the motor of evolutionary progress—is certainly not clear here, and presumably awaited clear formnlation on the part of the author. There is quite a sharp ideative gap separating *The Lord of the Sea* and *The Purple Cloud* from *The Last Miracle,* as well as a gap in time. Shiel may not have been ready in 1901 to carry through the philosophical thrust of *The Last Miracle.* (One must, however, be cautious on this point. The fact that *The Last Miracle* was not published until 1906 does not necessarily mean that it was not written until then—it is a highly controversial book which might have taken its time finding a willing publisher. Then again, there is internal textual evidence that the beginning and end of the book may have been separately written.)

In between The *Purple Cloud* and *The Last Miracle* Shiel published five novels, mostly riotous adventure stories with melodramatic plots. Only one is futuristic—the future war novel, *The Yellow Wave*. This features a war between Russia and Japan which threatens to disturb the sensible peace which most nations have accepted. The myth of the war to end war is no longer apparent here, as it was in *The Yellow Danger*, and the crude social Darwinism of the earlier book has quite disappeared. The war is ended not by genocide, nor even by victory, but by pacification in consequence of the tragedy of two young lovers, Yoshhio (son of the Japanese warlord) and Nadine (daughter of a Russian prince), who are killed when caught between the contending forces. One can see here an echo of the tragedy of *Romeo and Juliet*, a story which Shiel quoted more than once as the archetype of the *genuinely* happy ending—happy, that is, for the future of the world rather than for the fortunes of individuals. The purposes of this essay are, however, best served by passing quickly over *The Yellow Wave* to a detailed consideration of *The Last Miracle*.

As *The Purple Cloud* is Shiel's best book, largely for reasons unconnected with his philosophical development, so *The Last Miracle* might be reckoned just about his worst. It hangs together badly, has a plot which moves (when it moves at all) by virtue of the stupidities of its leading characters, and suffers such a wrenching change of perspective as it approaches its climax that most readers cannot help but feel cheated.

This time, the narrator of the story is not its hero, but simply a man who tags along—a Watsonian figure who really (from an aesthetic point of view) ought not to be in the plot at all. He tells of how his friend Aubrey Langler finds a wren with a message attached to its leg—an appeal for help issued by a priest imprisoned in the Austrian province of Styria. Although the message has not survived in its entirety Langler is able to determine that the man responsible for the outrage must be Baron Kolar, who is currently in England taking a keen interest in the career of a charismatic preacher.

Langler foolishly tells Kolar what he knows, and Kolar warns him to keep out of the affair. One of the warnings which he issues consists of driving knives through the hands of Langler's sister.

While Langler hesitates, a vision of the crucified Christ appears in a local Church—part of a series of miracles which touch off a revival of faith throughout Europe. The preacher, Barton, becomes a powerful force in British politics as a result of the new religious movement, and leads the opposition against a eugenics bill which will provide for the sterilization of "diseased persons."

Langler, being one of the few people in his parish who did not witness the miracle, is one of the few prepared to doubt it, and suspects that Kolar (who considers the eugenics bill far too moderate) somehow, and for some unknown reason, may have had a hand in it. Despite the violent warning, he sets off for Styria to secure the freedom of the imprisoned clergyman, but finds the task beyond him. Once the matter is brought to a conclusion (unsatisfactory, from his point of view), he returns to England for a final confrontation with Kolar, whose plans are reaching their climax.

Kolar has staged all the miracles on which the revived faith is founded, and plans to destroy the credibility of the Christian Churches once and for all with this revelation. (This scheme is parallel to the one featured in Guy Thorne's best-selling *When It Was Dark* [1904], where faked evidence that Christ's resurrection never took place precipitates such a crisis of faith that civilization totters and almost collapses.) Langler, in threatening this plan, is simply a minor nuisance, but instead of having him murdered the Baron volunteers to face him in a game of Russian Roulette employing two pills, one of which is poison. Thus, fate is to decide the path of the future—whether the world should go the way of credulity or scepticism.

So far, the reader has been encouraged to believe that Langler is the hero of the book and Kolar its villain. It has been revealed that Kolar had good reason for wanting to be revenged on the priest he imprisoned, but he has taken that revenge in such a monstrous fashion as to alienate any sympathy which might have accrued to his credit. Now, though, the author shows his true hand and reveals that he has been bluffing: Kolar, after all, is on the right side, and Langler is an unfortunate meddler who has made of himself an obstruction to progress. Langler dies, and his injured sister soon follows him, but the consequences of Kolar's victory are displayed in an enthusiastic appendix which leaps forward into the future to describe the new religious order which arises out of the ashes of Christianity: the Church-of-the-Overman.

Here—in a section not without its ironies and with a rather uncharacteristic element of satire—we learn that men have not lost their religion because of Kolar, but rather have found it:

> It is just beginning to be religious. Religion is a modern thing like electrometers. Not that Plato, Jesus, the caveman, were not religious a little in their villager-way, but our religion is a river to their trickle: they hadn't our data, our means, to be religious. Isn't religion an attitude of adoration and donation? the donation depending upon the adoration? the adoration depending upon knowledge of the Being adored, upon science? Adoration is a compound of (1) awe, and (2) love; and to have it we must know that God is (1) great, and (2) greatly good. But no ancient could suspect these: Jesus believed that the stars would some day "fall from heaven," and that God is littley good, "loving" village Tom and Dick; *we* know The Gospel, The Tidings of Great Joy, that (1) the stars are suns, (2) that we come from monkeys. Our stars can't "fall" upon Jerusalem "like figs": a thousand million earths can fall into Betelgeuse and be lost, and there are doubtless billions of billions of Betelgeuses in a billion island-universes, of which a few are visible to our eye-pieces. God's great: we have awe. And we are related to snakes: there is a principle of progress in Being leading on to lives that will one day be finer, wiser, more wildly delighted, than ever entered into our little hearts to fancy. Now, how greatly good—Ah, the glad tidings!—we can't help loving: we have adoration. And from adoration springs donation, which is religion in the stricter use—that which "binds us back" from living to please our roughest upper-self: so the village-religions said "live to please the neighbours, Tom, Dick." But the evolution of this? Is it not "live to please the distant, invisible: Man, Society?" And the evolution of this? Is it not "live to please even the non-existent, the still unborn?"[9]

The narrator hears this argument from a friend, and visits a church at his exhortation to watch a ritual and film show, in which one key element is a new version of the parable of the good Samaritan. This serves to exemplify the important last part of the above argument, forming the basis for Shiel's particular view of morality: his own particular theory of "the good," which underlies and explains many of the peculiarities in his novels.

The parable runs as follows:

> In a grim gorge we saw a man named Adamson robbed by brigands, left bleeding; after which a broker passed along in haste, casting glances of alarm, saw Adamson, but did not stop. Then came a scientist—young, strong-looking, inclined to baldness—frowning over a phial, till he caught sight of Adamson: upon which he stopped his carriage, and with a look of annoyance was getting out, when a rattle of brigands galloping somewhere reached his ears: whereupon, muttering "No, thank you," he was again on in haste. And now comes the good Samaritan trotting on an ass, a squat Sancho Panza: he, seeing the wounded, muttered "My goodness, that poor man...how, should *I* feel?," while tears filled his eyes. He was soon putting oil and wine on Adamson's wounds, heaving Adamson upon the ass, leading him to an inn within the pass...At that inn, too, the scientist put up: and there we witnessed both his death and Adamson's, who died after five days: for oil and wine are not the right things to put on wounds, and the good Samaritan's oil and wine teemed with bacteria, which were exhibited magnified on the screen: so that Adamson died in agony. So did the scientist: for, experimenting on toxins, serums, antiseptics, he injected himself, conscious that it might end him. and writhing he died, writing down the result of the experiment. We marked the holy martyr's immolation of himself with hcarts that smarted, yet with an exultance which soared on wings of joy—I say "we," for throughout all the enormousness of that hall a storm of acclamation reigned. Then another scene: a battlefield: Adamsons wounded in tens of thousands: and most of them the scientist's antiseptic rescued. And now the last scene: a village graveyard: the good Samaritan's tombstone: marked on it "He was a good neighbour"; then the scientist's statue atop of a column: and the column moved up, and up, and up, across the screen, so that its top seemed to reach the very heavens; and it was suggested that roaring round its base was a noising as of many waters, voices of ten thousand times ten thousand raised in adoration; and on its base was marked "Servant of God, Neighbour of Men."[10]

This makes the point abundantly clear. The religiosity of the Christian churches is out of date, according to Shiel. In learning more about the universe we have learned more about God, and must take this into account in our worship. The new knowledge must be the foundation-stone of a new morality in which our responsibilities are very much wider. The fact that a man like Kolar treats his neighbors very badly—even injuring and killing them—will not win our acclaim, but does not in itself warrant our condemnation. He must be judged, also if not instead, by the consequences of his actions as they affect millions of people, including millions not yet born. It is what he does for *progress,* for the evolution of mankind, that *really* counts.

THE POLITICS OF EVOLUTION: M. P. SHIEL

According to Shiel we have the wrong heroes and the wrong saints. We revere the wrong kind of martyr. In the moral theory sanctified by Shiel's idea of God and His goodness what happens to individuals really does not matter much, and what individuals do to one another does not matter either, if it is done in the service of a much greater good: the furtherance of science and the cause of progress.

This is reflected in Shiel's work in several ways: directly, in the elevation to heroic status of men like Kolar and Dr. Krasinski in *Dr. Krasinski's Secret* (1929); and indirectly, in the author's attitude toward his heroes. It now becomes clear why his heroes can behave like idiots in personal matters, and how they can be treated cruelly by fate as regards the failure of their projects and the manner of their deaths. What they do, and what happens to them, must properly be evaluated in terms of a much larger scheme of things: the scheme of progress. As individuals, they and their personal affairs are of no importance; as pieces in a greater game, they may have a contribution to make. Langler, the good Samaritan, turns out to be a black pawn, while Kolar is a white piece; in the game it matters not what they think of themselves or what their neighbors think of them.

Superficially, it may seem that there is a return in *The Last Miracle* to the crude social Darwinism of *The Yellow Danger*, especially in respect of the bill for the sterilization of the unfit. Shiel's attitude to this is ambiguous—though Kolar approves and Langler thinks it a bestial and sinful thing, it is not necessarily so that Kolar's is *the* view which receives the final endorsement. The point to be made, however, is that according to Shiel, the justification such actions would require has nothing to do with Darwinism at all, even in a crude analogical sense. To call Shiel a social Darwinist at this stage of his career would be to mistake the whole context of his thinking. His view of evolution is very different from Darwin's: it is an aspect of Being, and God is *within* it. Far from being a process in which order arises from the operation of natural selection on spontaneous mutation, Shiel's evolution is an ascent of mind, as vital in the life of the universe as the arrow of time itself.

The epilogue of The *Last Miracle* features Shiel's first literary use of the concept of the "overman." He uses the word frequently, mainly because of a strong dislike (on etymological grounds) for the word "superman." This is explained in a footnote to the original version of "On Reading" omitted in the version in *Science, Life and Literature*. The same footnote[11] makes reasonably clear the sense in which he was at that point using it. He refers to several "men of educated consciousness," including H. G. Wells, George Bernard Shaw, and—perhaps most significantly—the poet John Davidson. He constructs an imaginary dialogue in which Davidson is entitled to answer criticism of his recent work (presumably the five *Testaments,* though no title is given) by claiming to possess such an educated consciousness, and thus to qualify as an overman. The etymological note acknowledges that the word is a translation of Nietzsche's *übermensch,* but the probability is that Shiel got it from Nietzsche *via* Davidson rather than direct.

Shiel's reasons for borrowing the term "overman" were sound enough, but his use of the term can be misleading to the unwary reader, especially if one overestimates the importance of the concept in his thinking. The blurb attached to the Mycroft & Moran collection, *Prince Zaleski and Cummings King Monk,* claims that "Throughout his life M. P. Shiel was obsessed by the notion of the 'Overman,' the precursor to a new and superior race that he beieved would gradually evolve under the benison of modern science. Zaleski and Monk embody in essence the fictional adaptation of this superhuman sensibility." In fact, though, there is little evidence that Shiel was "obsessed" with the notion of the overman, and the talk of a "new and superior race" is surely misleading when one recalls that the sole qualification for being an overman is an educated consciousness.

The main reason why Shiel's use of the term gives the wrong impression (through no fault of his own!) is that nobody else has ever adopted the word. Because it is clearly taken from Nietzsche, it can easily seem that Shiel is using it in the same way that Nietzsche used *übermensch*. This is certainly not so: the moral philosophies of Shiel and Nietzsche are actually polar opposites.

Whether Shiel ever actually read Nietzsche is difficult to know. He casually lets fall the names of many philosophers in *Science, Life and Literature*, but Nietzsche's is not among them. It appears in the footnote to the original "On Reading," but is misspelled. John Davidson, whose work shows very strong Nietzschean influences, may well have provided Shiel with all the contact he had with Nietzschean ideas.

The point is that Nietzsche's moral philosophy is very highly individualist. For Nietzsche, the only people who really *matter,* in the human world, are those rare individuals possessed of the power of creativity—men of genius. Unfortunately (in Nietzsche's view) civilization and the prevailing morality are the creations of gregarious weaklings, who have created a world dominated by "the ethics of the herd." The morally transformed world of the *übermensch* is yet to appear.

Shiel also looks forward to a moral transformation of society—*The Last Miracle* makes this abundantly clear—but Shiel is the ultimate moral collectivist. For him, individuals hardly matter at all as *individuals.* Men of genius are celebrated only for their contribution to the commonweal. Shiel's overmen are already among us, and they can be created relatively easily; Nietzsche's overmen are so rare and ultimately precious that it is not clear from his writings whether any one of them has yet walked the earth.

There are, of course, similarities between Shiel and Nietzsche, but the similarities conceal vital points of difference. Both were opposed to the Christian Churches, and mounted virulent attacks upon them, but Nietzsche actually despised the moral teachings of Christ, whereas Shiel merely thought that it was time for a higher moral consciousness to be imposed upon them, as an extension rather than a reversal. Then again, both Nietzsche and Shiel exhibit a seeming moral callousness, considering murder a relatively trivial affair which might easily be justified—but the arguments they would have given in justification are crucially different. Nietzsche's *übermensch* is entitled to do as he likes simply because of what he is; Shiel's overman may use others cynically only if he is working in the great cause of science and progress, working for the future of mankind.

Shiel's notion of the overman is made clearer in the novel in which he describes the deliberate creation of an overman by a process of unusual education, *The Isle of Lies*, which was published in 1909—the same year as *This Knot of Life*.

The Isle of Lies is the story of Hannibal Lepsius, the son of an archaeologist who has him conceived and then shapes his upbringing for the sole purpose of deciphering fifteen mysterious ideographs at the end of an inscription engraved on a stele, which he has stolen from an Abyssinian monastery. (The archaeologist is presumably named in honor of Karl Richard Lepsius, the German Egyptologist who helped to found modern scientific archaeology.)

Hannibal Lepsius is reared on an Island by his father and a single assistant, Shan Healy (his mother having conveniently died after giving birth). There he is made to believe that the world at large is inhabited by men of great intellect and perfect physique. Healy, a man of no mean intelligence, is represented as a person of contemptible stupidity, while Lepsius senior works hard to maintain the illusion that he is a much greater genius than in fact he is. Hannibal, in the full flower of youth, is expected to be stronger and quicker than his teachers, who lay down "normal" standards which they, regretfully, cannot attain. The fraud is successful—belief is all that is required for Hannibal Lepsius to make himself into an overman such as the world has not yet seen.

The project comes to fruition when the scientist finally gives the stele to his son and demands a translation. The boy gets as far as the man was able to, but then falters. He takes the stele away in order to consider the problem, but he never returns. Visitors have come, by chance, to the island, and Hannibal is carried away by a sudden passion on first seeing a woman. The woman in question is a lady's maid named Jeanne Auvache, who is attractive to him solely because he has seen no other woman to compare her to. She smuggles him aboard the yacht which brought her, after he recklessly proposes marriage.

Hannibal soon finds out that there are more beautiful women in the world than Jeanne Auvache—and he soon finds, too, that his expectations of civilization are wildly inaccurate. He falls in love all over again, with Jeanne's mistress Eve Vickery, but is soon parted from her when he is forced to flee England after a brush with the law.

After a gap of some years we meet Lepsius again, now more-or-less adapted to the world as it is. He has settled in France, and is trying to raise capital in the Bourse to finance a bold project in high technology—the launching of an artificial satellite which will (apparently) illuminate the Earth as a new moon. His plans apparently go well beyond this—a letter which he is presumed to have written hints at the intention to rule the world—but we learn no details. He is distracted from his scheming by the arrival in France of Eve Vickery. Although she is now affianced, he renews his suit with rigor. He is a lonely man because the entire race "suppurates in dullness," and he longs for a partner to educate to something near his own level.

Hannibal's enemies seize the opportunity of his infatuation with Eve to set traps for him. He abducts her, lodging her in his house at Serapis, and seems to have confounded the plans laid against him. The legacy of his past errors, though, brings him down. The deserted Jeanne Auvanche has vowed to vitriolize him, and has once failed to do so. Now, at last, she succeeds in taking her revenge, and blinds him. He is destroyed and his plans for world-improvement collapse, but by an ironic twist of fate it is this destruction, which teaches him humility, that at last makes him acceptable to Eve Vickery, who takes him to her bosom.

The naive reader will take the ending of *The Isle of Lies* to be a happy one, with its triumph of sentiment and affection over vaulting ambition. By Shiel's standards, it should rather be reckoned a tragedy, for the world remains unimproved. Actually, as with Kolar, one suspects a certain ambivalence in Shiel's attitude, as if he were reluctant at this stage to take his ideas to their logical conclusion. It is too easy, reading *The Last Miracle*, to see Kolar as an out-and-out villain even at the end; similarly, it is too difficult to accept Hannibal Lepsius wholeheartedly as a hero. When he mentions casually to Eve that his motives for creating a world-state are not entirely selfless, but reflect in part a desire to play in godlike fashion with the lives of men, and that he does not much care if millions die in the pursuit of his ends, one is rather inclined to sympathize with her horror; nor does Shiel work hard to prevent our doing so.

Lepsius is the only character in Shiel's scientific romances who is enough of an overman to despise contemporary science in the same way that his ordinarily educated men despise the limitations of ancient knowledge. Because of this, though, he seems to have lost the sympathy of the author in some degree, and Shiel seems to concur in the opinion that he really does *need* to learn a measure of humility. It is significant that though his father eliminates any mention of religion from his education, the younger Lepsius later finds a certain fascination in the life of Jesus. Shortly before his blinding, when the first act of betrayal is about to begin his downfall, he is to be found reading the gospel according to St. Matthew. The news that actually sends Eve Vickery scurrying back to his side is that he has forgiven Jeanne Auvache. (It should be noted, though, that there are two ways to interpret this—Eve thinks that it means he has become a kind of Christian, but Shiel's overmen in general do not bear grudges because they recognize their own insignificance in the evolutionary schema.)

One probably should conclude that the ambivalence of *The Isle of Lies* represents a partial retreat from the philosophical standpoint assumed in the appendix to *The Last Miracle* (which seems itself to be slightly uneasy).

The Isle of Lies stands almost at the end of Shiel's first prolific period. After 1909 there was a three-year gap before his next novel, during which he published the short story collection, *The Pale Ape*. The next novel, *The Dragon*, was followed by an even longer gap. *The Dragon*, later retitled *The Yellow Peril*, seems to be a deliberate return to Shiel's beginnings as a novelist. It is a revisitation of the theme of *The Yellow Danger*, adapted to the changes which had overtaken the author's philosophy in the meantime. The ringing rhetoric of its last chapter presents a synthesis of the political philosophy of *The Lord of the Sea* and the "evolutionary theology" of *The Last Miracle*. There is no mention in it of overmen.

As in *The Yellow Danger*, we find in *The Dragon* an Oriental genius bent on world destruction and locked by circumstance into a personal duel with a particular Englishman. Here the whole war is essentially an extension of the personal feud, the Chinaman Li Ku Yu having been bested by the English Prince Teddy in a schoolboy scrap and having sworn to get even at *any* cost. The two combatants are each aided—or at least abetted—by their female partners, Li Ku Yu by the ingenious Oyone and Teddy by the commoner whom he has secretly married (and who remains blissfully unaware that she is wed to the heir to the throne!).

Although *The Dragon* cannot be said to be one whit more plausible than its preposterous predecessor, it makes much more interesting reading. It is a perfect melodrama: a remarkable blend of Cinderella and Fu Manchu, full of plots and fights, captures and escapes, mistaken identities and perilous misapprehensions. The weapons employed in the eventual international conflict are, as might be expected, more enterprising than those deployed in the earlier novel: a flying boat and a deadly ray play crucial roles.

Whereas the confrontation between yellow and white in *The Yellow Danger* was essentially a conflict between racial groups, the confrontation in *The Dragon* is represented as a clash between mind-sets. Even in the earlier novel the Chinese mind was castigated for its devotion to the tyranny of method and custom, and here again it is mocked on much the same grounds. Overall, though, the contest of argument is much more even-handed. Towards the end of the book, when Prince Teddy and Li Ku Yu have their climactic contest of wills, they spend a surprising amount of time agreeing about philosophical fundamentals. Li Ku Yu shoots out Shielian theses with which Teddy cannot disagree, and it is only at the very last that his train of argument is derailed:

> "What one thing is it that concerns living beings—that living
> beings care about? Happiness? Agreed?"
> "Yes."

"Good! And happiness consists in worshipping God? say in 'religion.' Agreed?"

"Yes."

"Good! Now, the scientist denies that apes, negroes, bishops, bouzis, dervishes, are religious; denies that anyone can possibly be religious—but him; since no one else can have any knowledge of God—but him; denies that anyone knows what religion *is* but him. And he is right—necessarily! Agreed?"

"Yes."

"Good! Now, at my birth I observe two masses of men, equal in number—one white one yellow; both having what they call 'a religion'; but the brain of the yellow much more disengaged from his 'religion,' equally superstitious, but less deformed and diseased with superstition, less incapable of being led to look in a centric sane mood at the universe, and be truly religious. So said I to myself: 'The European brain will take two hundred years to evolve out of the notion that Christianity has some connection with religion, resemblance to'; and if one answer, 'but already France Germany, England have rejected Christianity,' *I* answer back: 'they think so!' but for many days their mentation will be infected by the fact that for ages their fathers entertained the conceit that a mammal of their species, with 300 rudimentary organs, was the Infinite Itself. Imagine the astonishment of a zoologist of Mars to know that on some planet in space there paces an animal into whose head the disease of a conceit so *ec*-centric could creep and fester. Man? Comic! the laughing-stock of the cosmos! So said I: 'Save mankind two hundred years! abolish Europe.'"[12]

To which the Prince's response is "Well said"—and *then* comes the objection that Li Ku Yu has no proof whatever that the Chinese are more nearly capable of discovering God's truth than the men of the West, and that this is an unjustified assumption. Li Ku Yu has no *proof* to offer, and hence the matter must remain subject to test. This is what the war is really about. The Oriental forces are, of course, defeated—though some readers might think that the miraculous ray-gun which turns the trick is a trifle arbitrary as a method—and the hero's triumph is for once unmarred by any personal tragedy. (Given that he is the future king of England, for Shiel to mistreat him as he usually mistreats his heroes would seem almost to be a species of treason.)

Like *The Last Miracle*, *The Dragon* has an epilogue, in which a kind of judgment is passed. It is set against the background of a universal anxiety precipitated by the knowledge that the Earth is to pass through the tail of a comet, but instead of disaster following, the groundwork is laid for a moral renewal of human civilization—not in any miraculous fashion, as in Wells's *In the Days of the Comet*, but by virtue of Teddy taking advantage of the receptiveness of his people to deliver a stirring speech whose message strikes home.

Teddy's edict begins by declaring Britain to be his own private property, "by right of conquest," so that social reforms can be imposed immediately. The nation is henceforth to devote itself to education and research, its citizens each having the duty to maintain a *mens sana in corpore sano* (somewhat after the fashion of the Samurai in Wells's *A Modern Utopia*). Teddy exhorts his fellow men to rigorous scepticism and keen curiosity. "Wake Up, England!" is his message, though he means something very different by it than the august ancestor he is quoting. He goes on in a more metaphysical vein, explaining his notion of God as the motivating force of the universe, immanent in everything.

By means of this inspiration, Teddy hopes to prove Li Ku Yu wrong, and to demonstrate that it is on the men of the West—specifically, the English—on whom the mantle of evolutionary proficiency will fall. It is tempting to regard this note of cheerful optimism as an indicator of the fact that Shiel had for the time being summarized his position fully, and had nothing more to add.

Children of the Wind, which appeared ten years after *The Dragon,* is a Haggardesque adventure story in which a remote African tribe is ruled by a white woman who is also an heiress. Her cousin comes to take her home in order to claim her inheritance, but brings in tow her deadly enemy, who must kill her in order to become the beneficiary himself. Although there is a little philosophical discussion about progress, civilization, and happiness at the beginning of the book, it is quickly curtailed when the action starts. In respect of the development of Shiel's ideas, the one really interesting inclusion in the story is an argument concerning the justification of war, which Shiel later made the basis of his essay "Of the Necessity of War," in *Science, Life and Literature* (though the notes there locate its true origin as early as 1915).

The argument in the essay is complicated, but is basically muddled social Darwinism. The impulse to make war, it is argued, arises out of a subconscious awareness that numbers are outstripping resources (in a particular ecological context). War is thus inevitable, but is also sometimes good given appropriate social institutions. The fact that the best males are wasted in combat is eugenically bad, but can be compensated for, in Shiel's view, by the fact that *provided there is monogamy,* the shortage of men will result in the worst of the women being eliminated from the breeding stock. Shiel appears to have believed that this is more than simply a restoration of the eugenic balance, because he was of the opinion (derived, it appears, from Schopenhauer) that it is from their mothers that men receive their intellectual powers. As evolution, for the Spencerian Shiel, is primarily a matter of the evolution of intelligence, it therefore follows that eliminating the poorer women from the breeding population is much more important than preserving the best men. Why it was that Shiel, the passionate advocate of scepticism, should have accepted this astonishing argument remains unclear. It does, however, crop up elsewhere in his work, and there seems little doubt that he did take it quite seriously.

The reluctance to interrupt a fast-moving plot with philosophical discussion does not show up at all in the second novel Shiel wrote after his comeback, *How the Old Woman Got Home,* which is copiously equipped with situations which delay and distract the hero so that he can discourse at some length about abstract matters, summarizing Shiel's intellectual position. Shiel seems to have been pleased with this accomplishment, and though confessing that he had a kinder memory of *Children of the Wind,* draws attention to the later novel in the final version of his oft-rewritten essay, "Of Myself":

> But the *Old Woman* one has this distinction, that in it is given, so to say, my political system. I first demonstrate what "good" means—and anyone who makes quite sure of this little thing will be astonished at the flood of light which it will throw into his thoughts on all sorts of other subjects. I demonstrate, then, that the noun *"Good"* means pleasure, that the adjective "good" means pleasant—and nothing else. Then I demonstrate that *all* pleasure, *all* good, is the result of truth, of science—the science of the amoeba or of Newton. Then I demonstrate that the

growth of truth, of science, of pleasure, of Good, depends (1) upon brains (a little), and (2) upon luck (much). Then I demonstrate that, though the luck of a million is exactly a millionfold more than the luck on one, the million must be *in the way* of truth seeking truth, or no luck can accrue—must be scientists, men of leisure; but this they can't be, if they are slaves, i.e., "landless men," men without a country: so that any great growth of Good depends upon countries being owned by nations.[13]

Caxton Hazlitt's expanded version of all this is much more detailed and slightly more sophisticated than the version contained in Prince Teddy's speech at the end of *The Dragon*, but in essence the message has not changed at all. The socialist argument, plugging Hogarth's Georgian ideas, is put much more completely and in stronger terms, and for the first time we have a full elaboration of the role of sheer luck in the advancement of science; but there is nothing new about the fundamentals of the case. Some of the details represent new "discoveries" on Shiel's part—for instance, he dismisses Einstein's theory of relativity in rather cavalier fashion as a folly unworthy of serious intellectual consideration—but it is arguable that the most interesting feature of the novel is Shiel's choice of Caxton Hazlitt as his mouthpiece.

Hazlitt is an impoverished man, unable to find work or to make use of his talents, but he is by training an engineer—a man of practical scientific knowledge. (Shiel valued practical expertise highly, rather more than abstract theoretical understanding.) He lays claim, at one point, to the title of overman. And yet, insofar as his projects within the plot are concerned, he is a hopeless incompetent. He allows himself to be deluded, distracted, and all-but-destroyed by his adversaries. Such successes as his cause does enjoy are due to the enterprise and energy of his devoted friends (who are far from being overmen, being almost completely ignorant). When, in the end, he fails to achieve his goals, he gives way to a deathly depression, will not allow himself to be redeemed by the girl who loves him and is carrying his unborn child, and commits suicide.

This seems perverse, and in a sense it is, but there is calculation within the perversity. We usually expect that the characters who embrace an author's doctrines—and thus become his heroes, his surrogate selves—will be rewarded for their servitude. It is, after all, an author's prerogative to determine how things fall out within his plots, and to distribute rewards and punishments as he pleases. When an author chooses to subject those who hold to his doctrines to every humiliation at his command, this seems almost to constitute a treason against his own ideas. We must not lose sight, though, of the kind of doctrine that Shiel and his heroes embrace. Within the context of thought sketched out above it makes perfect sense that an overman need not be a successful man: he is not a Nietzschean *übermensch* or a Carlylean hero; he is merely a participant in a general progress which is largely a *haphazard* process in which there are many casualties. The personal tragedy of Caxton Hazlitt is quite irrelevant to the ideative issues which are really at stake in *How the Old Woman Got Home*. It is completely detached from the question of whether the conclusion of the story is "good" or "happy" in Shiel's eccentric uses of those terms; it is a separate matter.

It is perhaps in this novel rather than any other where one has to bear in mind Shiel's notion of a happy ending. There is an argument in the connecting material of the short story collection, *Here Comes the Lady* (published one year after *How the Old Woman Got Home* in 1928), which forms the basis for one of the briefest essays in *Science, Life and Literature*. Here it is argued that all tales should end happily, but that an ending which leaves the characters contented and rich is happy only in a very trivial sense. *Real* happy endings are those which—like *Romeo and Juliet*—end happily for the greater society. The ending of *How the Old Woman Got Home* does promise to be happy in this way: in giving up the fortune to which he is entitled, Caxton Hazlitt asks that it be used in the cause of progress and enlightenment.

This lesson has also to be borne in mind while reading *Dr. Krasinski's Secret*, which followed *How the Old Woman Got Home* in 1929. Here, too, a fortune is at stake, and the eponymous scientist is determined to acquire it by marriage, clearing out of the way the contenders who stand in line ahead of his intended bride. His instrument in committing these murders is a young boy whom he imprisons and forces to become addicted to alcohol; the boy is a carrier of a deadly disease. The story is cool and clinical, reflecting the personality of its anti-hero, who appears for most of the plot to be the perfect Gothic villain in modern guise, but whose cause is eventually endorsed. Krasinski is not allowed to carry through his scheme to its conclusion, but after his death it is another scientist who marries the heiress, and the fortune is put to proper use. Here again we discover the only real happy ending that was possible within the framework of the plot, in Shiel's terms.

In his second productive phase Shiel produced only one long scientific romance. This was his last published novel, *The Young Men Are Coming* (1937). Although not the best-written of his books, this is the most ambitious of his speculative fictions, and one of his most important works.

The Young Men Are Coming is the story of Dr. Oscar Warwick, an aging scientist who makes accidental contact with alien beings landed temporarily on Earth. He is taken for a ride in their spacecraft, and sees many marvellous things. The high point of his visit is a long discussion with an unborn alien, which is sentient, intelligent, and communicative despite the fact that it is not yet hatched from its egg. When the aliens bring him home he has two souvenirs of the contact: a vague promise of future help if he should call and if his call should be heard; and the elixir of life.

Rejuvenation completely changes his character, filling him with a new verve and a desperate enthusiasm for changing the world. On a mad whim he "elopes" with his son's girl-friend, taking advantage of the fact that she mistakes his identity. This petty indulgence sows the seeds of disaster: he makes a bitter enemy of the girl's father, shatters the girl's life when he quickly deserts her (leaving her pregnant), and annoys his deserted wife, Felicia. All three consequences extend through the plot, entangling its motions.

In London, Warwick adopts the name of Wallace, and founds a social movement called the Young Men. This has such an influence with young disaffected idealists that it quickly begins to pose a political threat to the Establishment. The government, in response, prepares for repressive action and totalitarian rule. Wallace becomes involved in a feud with an evangelist, which he boldly offers to settle by a contest of miracle-working, where each man will try to whip up a storm. The evangelist is let down by his paternalistic God, but Wallace succeeds only too well with the aid of his alien apostles of science: *their* storm all but wrecks the world. In the meantime, the Young Men have risen in arms against the government, and Wallace discovers a personal obsession as fierce as his renewed youth will permit—his love for the beautiful Caroleth Lavarock (who is, unknown to him, his wife Felicia, who has discovered his store of the elixir).

Warwick/Wallace is basically a new version of Hannibal Lepsius, combining all the accumulated knowledge and understanding of a long lifetime's dedication to science with preternaturally vigorous youth and health. Like the young Lepsius, he is threatened with defeat as a result of an unthinking slight against a woman, but he is *not* brought down in the end. In this story a perverse ending is not required to emphasize Shiel's conviction about the relative importance of individuals and the common good, because it contains an inserted parable more effective even than the rewritten tale of the good Samaritan. Wallace hears at one point about a valuable experiment in brain surgery that is deemed too dangerous to be carried out. He immediately volunteers himself as a subject for this vivisection, and is allowed to deliver himself fearfully to his presumed destruction before the surgeon, thinking to teach the young man a lesson, turns contemptuously away. Wallace, though, is angered rather than relieved by his release, and determines to carry out the operation himself. He has no difficulty in finding a volunteer from the ranks of the Young Men, but has not the skill for the delicate work, and concedes that his botched attempt has been sheer murder. The fact that the experiment fails only serves to hammer home the moral that the true overman is ever-ready to disregard his own personal safety when the good of the commonweal is at stake. This might be reckoned the ultimate example of the "negative paranoia" so characteristic of Shielian heroes.

More than any other of Shiel's scientific romances The *Young Men Are Coming* discusses actual scientific theory and possibility. In his essay in *This Knot of Life* he spoke of the necessity of being well-read in science, but never in the first phase of his career did he ever demonstrate any familiarity with contemporary scientific knowledge and theory. Here, though, the dialogue with the egg and the hero's occasional soliloquies provide Shiel with the means to display his opinions of the science of the day.

Shiel is adamant here, and in *Science, Life and Literature,* that the concept of absolute motion is neither metaphysical (as Maxwell believed) nor wrong (as Einstein maintained). Thus he defends the classical theory of Newton against its modern detractors. He is equally cavalier in his dimissal of several other contemporary theories, notably the nebular theory of the origin of the solar system (his arguments here seem much more sound). Newton gets less support in the matter of gravitational theory, when the egg contemptuously rejects the idea that every particle in the universe attracts every other, and goes on to "explain" gravity as an electromagnetic phenomenon. This becomes elaborated into an astonishing metaphysical system in which the interplay of positive and negative charges is considered to be a manifestation of a kind of universal sexuality. The egg is just as expert in metaphysics as in physics, and it is no surprise to find it holding to the Shielian theology in which God is Force—the inherent motion of the universe. As a moral philosopher, the egg is also an orthodox follower of Shiel, the good being deemed synonymous with pleasure and with cleverness according to the customary reconstruction of these terms. All this rests on the usual bedrock of evolutionary theory:

> A *low* society, then, is one in which some of the folk are not engaged on science, on doubting and discovering, on truth: for science is *the good* of Life, the *only* good; but some of the folk are engaged in working to earn a livelihood, or to earn riches, working, not for Society, but for themselves, like cows: so that all that *luck* in science, that *luck* in discovering and doubting, which is special to each of these workers for self, as to no other life, is lost to Society: lost all the eventfulness and elation of their inventing! And in such environments the climb of Life could not be balked, since such environments exalt the slowest lives; but Life wriggles

95

free by that trick of God through which, in spite of all, Life is at all times climbing, this trick consisting in quickening Life at its spring, continuously: for in conception it is the quickest spermion which spurts into the ovum, the multitude of other spermia which run the race perishing; and the individual who originates from the quickest spermion has spermia whose average of quickness is as high, the quickest of these being quicker still, inheriting a stress as well as a strength: and so on. In this way the *physical* quickness of Life is continuously heightened; and since the ovum's quickness increases step for step with the spermion's, so, too, does the psychic quickness of Life increase continuously: for since Life is female, and Mind is the trait of Life, our *mind* is from the ovum, from our mothers.[14]

Much of this is later repeated, for emphasis, by Wallace in convincing others of the worthiness of his cause. The difference between "young" and "old" as they are employed in the story is, of course, subsumed within this system of ideas. The old are slow and "low"; youth is not a matter of chronology but of *vitality* in every sense of the word. The old know more, but it is the young who are *seeking* to know, responsible therefore for the activity and discovery that adds to the sum of human knowledge and the level of social evolution.

We should remember, in reading this, that Shiel was 72 when *The Young Men Are Coming* was published, and that he had not health and strength enough to prepare another book for publication. The novel is, in part, a dream fantasy whose personal significance should not be underestimated. It is also the story which, by offering the fullest account of Shiel's opinions about physics and metaphysics, most fully exposes his vulnerability as a man of ideas. Where he makes empirical claims these are almost invariably unfounded, and his arguments are often fatally flawed (it does not take much ingenuity to see the error in his pseudo-Darwinian case for a perennial increase in the sprinting speed of sperms). One is inclined to reflect, with a full appreciation of the irony thereof, that Shiel was wise to place so much stress on the role of luck in scientific inquiry. His bad luck can thus be discounted as an inevitability: he becomes merely another casualty of the randomness with which chance distributes its rewards. In the end, Shiel was a Shielian hero himself, his personal mission frustrated.

To a considerable extent, the concerns of M. P. Shiel were the common concerns of the more serious writers of early British scientific romance. He wrote several future war stories and one disaster story. He was interested in evolutionary philosophy and socialism. He was deeply suspicious of the hold which religious ideas had over the minds of his contemporaries. One could say the same of Wells and of Beresford, modifying hardly a word. To all these matters, however, he brought a determined idiosyncrasy of viewpoint which isolated him as a writer.

Although Shiel's particular complex of ideas was his alone, the individual parts of it were firmly rooted in nineteenth-century thought. More often than not, they were rooted in aspects of nineteenth-century thought that were themselves eccentric and which have since lost fashion and credibility. Shiel's economics is the economics of Henry George rather than of Marx; his evolutionism is the evolutionism of Spencer rather than of Darwin. Even his dogged insistence on being reckoned a deist rather than an agnostic or an atheist cannot conceal the fact that his anti-clericalism is allied to the ideas of Thomas Henry Huxley, Auguste Comte, and Ludwig Feuerbach. Thirty-seven years of living in the twentieth century had not shaken Shiel's commitment to these ideas when he summarized his position in *The Young Men Are Coming*. No doubt he would have wanted to be reckoned a Young Man in spirit, but in fact he had not escaped from the trap of age.

The genuinely original aspect of Shiel's philosophical system is to be found in his social and moral philosophy. The character of his commitment to socialism is very different from Wells's commitment to Fabianism, and though he borrowed his economic theory from Henry George (or, perhaps, came to the same conclusion on his own), his political rhetoric is very different from George's.

For Shiel, the exploitation of the working classes by capitalists and landlords was not bad simply because it was exploitation. He was not at all interested in lifting the yoke of misery from the workers simply to make them *comfortable*. Exploitation was bad, for Shiel, in precisely the way that nineteenth-century religiosity was bad: *because it stifled scientific inquiry*. It was bad for the mind, rather than for the body. The injustice of the system was a minor matter, for Shiel; the suffering of individuals was of no consequence. What mattered was that evolution was being held back.

Shiel was a moral collectivist, but not in the usual sense. His collectivism did not follow from his socialism, nor was it the kind of collectivism frequently associated with Fascism. It arose independently, of itself: a pure conviction that the nation, the human race, the life of the universe, are what really matter, and individuals hardly at all. When Shiel tells us that *good* is synonymous with *pleasant*, he is not preaching hedonism or some variant of the creed of self-fullfilment: for him we can only speak of "good" and "right" in terms of whole societies—in terms of *the* whole Society.

Some readers have seen in Shiel's work a disturbing lack of moral order, but in fact they are simply failing to see what kind of moral order is there. For Shiel, there is never the slightest doubt that certain ends justify virtually any means, the ends in question being those specified by Spencerian evolutionary theory. (Though he occasionally voiced ideas which attract the label of "social Darwinism," this is probably to mistake the provenance of those ideas. In fact he was a Spencerian—to speak of a "social Spencerian" would be a pleonasm—of a slightly unorthodox stripe. One notes with ironic approval that A. Reynolds Morse's bibliography lists among Shiel's manuscripts an unpublished and unperformed play: "Herbert Spencer: A Comedy in One Act.")

We are, of course, perfectly free to decide that Shiel's brand of moral collectivism is itself an evil, and given that it is embedded in a highly suspect metaphysical system we might even be tempted to dismiss it as absurd, but we cannot say that it is incoherent or that Shiel was inconsistent in his advocacy of it. It is the presence of this underlying pattern of thought that enlivens so many of Shiel's plots, and makes them both fascinating and disturbing. More than any other leading figure in the history of British scientific romance, he presents an imaginative challenge to the reader. His work does not have the imaginative fertility of Wells's speculative fictions, but it is not so easy to take up an intellectual position relative to his: he is harder to engage in intellectual dialogue.

Most contemporary readers will not find Shiel a particularly attractive proposition. His prose, alien in its own day, is even more alien today with its convolutions and its labyrinthine wildness. His ideas, similarly alien in his own day, are similarly even more alien today. Perverse as it may seem to assert it, though, it is precisely for these reasons that he is a writer worth getting to know. He is an original, in thought and in method, and no one reading Shiel could possibly have his or her ideative horizons narrowed as a result. If everything he believed was either wrong or silly—well, one could say the same of Plato. Intellectual progress is a matter of trial and error (no matter what role one attributes to luck), and we can often learn as much by contemplating the errors and getting to know their inadequacies as we can by imbibing the truths which we do not need to interrogate so closely.

V.

GALACTIC HITCH-HIKER

THE SUDDEN RISE OF DOUGLAS ADAMS

Shakespeare informs us that some are born great, some achieve greatness, and some have greatness thrust upon them. The tripartite division does not apply with equal aptness to all kinds of greatness, but it has a rough-and-ready propriety in the case of best-selling writers. There are, indeed, ready-made best-sellers whose entry into the lists is automatic once they have deigned to set pen to paper—people whose fame has already been secured by the cinema, by TV, or by the accident of their having been born into the royal family; there are those whose best-selling status is hard-won, the result of building up a loyal following over the course of a long literary career; there are those upon whom best-sellerdom descends suddenly and unexpectedly, according to some mercurial whim of the reading public.

Douglas Adams, one of the few men capable of achieving consistent atypicality, fits neatly into none of these categories.

Adams's fame did precede his print debut in 1979, but that fame came from what is in this day and age an unusual source: the backwater of the mass media, radio (not, of course, Radio 1). Nor was it obvious that the popularity of *The Hitch-Hiker's Guide to the Galaxy* as a radio show could be translated into huge book sales, because the show had what is generally known as a "cult following"—which meant only that those people who did like it liked it a lot. Marketing the first of the three books which turned the Hitch-Hiker scripts into consecutive prose was not made any easier by the fact that it got so far and then just stopped, leaving the story to be continued in the second volume of the series, *The Restaurant at the End of the Universe* (1980).

By 1982, when *Life, the Universe and Everything* was published, no doubts remained about its market potential. By then *The Hitch-Hiker's Guide to the Galaxy* had become an item of modern folklore. Its translation to the TV screen—and its subsequent plundering by TV ads—may have helped it to acquire this status, but it was the role which certain of its key images and throwaway lines began to play in everyday conversation which actually signified its acceptance into the rhetoric of folk-wisdom.

A best-seller of the magnitude of *Life, the Universe and Everything* virtually guarantees the similar success of whatever follows, provided that it is in much the same vein. What actually followed was *The Meaning of Liff*, a book of silly definitions compiled in collaboration with John Lloyd. It sold well, as it was bound to do, but it failed conspicuously to make any significant contribution to the rhetoric of folk-wisdom. Adams retreated to safer ground, adding a fourth book to the Hitch-Hiker "trilogy": *So Long, and Thanks for All the Fish* (1984)—the first such book to be composed as a novel, not an adaptation of radio scripts.

In the context of a continuing career. however, this was really only a delaying move. There was not much else actually to be done with the Hitch-Hiker scenario, and now the more interesting loose ends had been tidied up there was no point at all in continuing. Greatness once achieved *can* become a thing of the past, if no new successes are recorded. It was necessary to come up with something new, which would not need to live on borrowed charm, and what Adams came up with was *Dirk Gently's Holistic Detective Agency* (1987), whose spectacular success was quickly followed by a sequel, *The Long Dark Tea-Time of the Soul* (1988).

Although they have not received universal critical acclaim—publication of the second volume of Dirk Gently's exploits called forth a particularly ruthless demolition job by a *Sunday Times* reviewer—these books do serve to demonstrate that Adams's career was by no means a flash in the pan, and that his humor is flexible enough to fit more than one literary template. This may be of vital importance to his future prospects because humor, as a species of creativity, is very difficult to sustain over long distances. Writers whose specialty is sentimentality or action-adventure may find it relatively easy to spin out their endeavors indefinitely, but humorists never do. Shakespeare (whose own abilities were multifarious) noted that *brevity* is the soul of wit, and though he did not appear to regard this as a tragedy, he was not in a position to appreciate the predicament of a man like Douglas Adams, who—at the ripe young age of thirty-six—must contemplate the prospect of spending half a lifetime being consistently funny. One can count on the fingers of one hand the number of writers who have actually managed that, and there would be at least a couple of fingers to spare.

As the expiring actor remarked, dying is easy; comedy is hard.

Douglas Adams's initial success was all the more surprising when one considers that it was for a long time considered axiomatic by publishers that funny science fiction didn't sell. This has little to do with any lack of clever humorists among writers of SF—who include such noted wits as Robert Sheckley, Bob Shaw, and David Langford—but much to do with the expectations of the SF audience. A sufficiently large fraction of the hard core of SF readers has always preferred a sense of wonder to a sense of humor, and has tended to regard irreverence as something vaguely sacrilegious. Funny SF has in the past seemed to many SF readers to be a send-up of the genre itself, and an implied criticism of their own interest in it.

To a considerable extent, of course, Adams's own following must lie outside the hard core of SF buyers, because best-selling status requires the loyalty of a broader public—but there is no question of his following lying *entirely* beyond the bounds of the SF community or consisting mainly of people who do find the projects and pretensions of SF essentially absurd. Although the Hitch-Hiker books can be read as a satire on SF, mocking its *clichés* and conventions, it would be silly to argue that they are no more than that, or that they are mainly interesting because that is what they do. They must have done far more than that to put their author where he is today.

There are certain hazards involved in analyzing comedy. Because analysis has to be done earnestly, there is something paradoxically clinical about the analytical project itself; and whatever conclusions one comes to are bound to seem dull and portentous by comparison with that which is to be explained. Comedy is fun; explanations of why jokes work are anything but funny. It is only natural that people who laugh at jokes should feel that investigation of why they have laughed is at best utterly irrelevant and at worst threatening—because once we become fully conscious of how and why we find things funny we might be prevented thereby from finding them funny in the future.

There is in fact an odd circularity about bringing analysis to bear on the kind of humor in which Douglas Adams specializes, because one of the things he constantly makes fun of is the business of analysis and the dogged hunt for answers to awkward questions. The most famous sequence in the Hitch-Hiker books involves the ultimate supercomputer's quest for the answer to the ultimate question (of "life, the universe and everything"), which turns out, of course, to be "42." If there is anything which is ruthlessly and repeatedly asserted by Adams's anecdotes and vignettes, it is that when you try to figure out what it all means, all you get is a poke in the ego. The final punchline of the series, credited as "God's Final Message to His Creation," is the last in a series of calculatedly extreme letdowns.

To become a commentator on Douglas Adams, therefore, is to play Krikkit on a very sticky wicket, and one can forecast with total confidence that the legions of American academics who make a living teaching SF will avoid him, on the grounds that their research work is much more comfortable when they stick to the less witty bits of Ursula K. Le Guin and Philip K. Dick. But fools rush in, as they say, where angels would not dirty their feet, and having long ago failed to qualify as an angel (I was okay on the theory but couldn't cope with the practical), I am inclined to say: what the hell...

To be frankly pompous about it, the humor of *The Hitch-Hiker's Guide to the Galaxy* is fundamentally bathetic in character. It moves metronomically from the sublime to the ridiculous, continually dissolving the grandiose into the banal.

This movement has an undeniable propriety in the context of the scientific enlightenment, whose world-view has moved the Earth and the history of mankind from the very center of Creation to a periphery so far out in the sticks that one could not possibly conclude otherwise than that in a hitch-hiker's guide to the galaxy it would be lucky to qualify for a one-word entry, and that would be only too likely to be a contemptuous put-down. The eponymous book, represented on radio and TV by the plummily laconic voice of Peter Jones, continually reminds us of this harsh lesson, as in the famous "Space is big..." monologue. So does the plot, which begins with the demolition of Earth to make way for a new hyperspatial bypass. So much for the Apocalypse: humankind becomes a redundant punctuation mark in an inconsequential sentence, whose erasure only matters if and when we find out that the white mice who commissioned the planet had something much bigger in mind than human delusions of significance. In the Adamsian worldview the legendary four horsemen, were they to arrive at all, would be far more worried about whether they ought to stop off for a hamburger before getting on with the job than anything to do with their actual work of destruction.

It hardly needs to be observed that underneath the jokiness this is really a rather bleak view of things. Indeed, were we to tabulate and evaluate the many extant species of *angst*, this one could sensibly be reckoned a low scorer in the reasons-to-be-cheerful stakes, making Heideggerian preoccupations with the inevitability of death look rather weak at the knees. On the other hand, it does come ready-equipped with the appropriate existentialist strategy for coping ("DON'T PANIC"), which at least has the virtue of being rather more succinct than any recipe for attaining the Age of Reason drawn up by Jean-Paul Sartre *et al.*

Given that the world-view of modern science provides such convincing back-up for Adams's assertions regarding our utter triviality, it is perhaps surprising that SF in general (whose supposed mission is, after all, to explore what lies at and beyond the horizons of the scientific imagination) usually goes in the opposite direction.

ALGEBRAIC FANTASIES & REALISTIC ROMANCES, by Brian Stableford

Like the wild optimists of science who are trying to put us back in the center of Creation with the aid of the Anthropic Principle (which leaps in cavalier fashion from the observation that if the universe were other than it is we wouldn't be here to observe it to the supposition that it must be the way it is because we are its observers), the wild optimists of genre SF are always trying to make us feel better about ourselves. Sometimes they come clean and simply tell us straight out that we are the race destined to rule the sevagram, but they are characteristically more subtle in packaging their human chauvinism to look seductive. They tell us that after all, we can still do our best, and will discover if we do that remarkable achievements are open to us; the humanists among them remind us that even if we can't conquer the universe at least we can explore the possibility of being nice to one another.

Douglas Adams is infinitely more cynical than such speculators as these, which is why he sometimes appears to be ruthlessly taking the piss out of them. In fact, though, he is simply telling it like it is, and one reason that it is funny is that if it *wasn't* funny it would be too horrid to contemplate. It is made all the funnier by the fact that Marvin the paranoid android is forever trying to point out to us that it really *isn't* funny, and that it *is* too horrid to contemplate.

The main problem with bathetic humor is that every time you move from the sublime to the ridiculous it gets harder to scale the heights of sublimity again. There comes a time when you have shot the last sacred cow in the herd, and there is nothing sufficiently grandiose left to be worth dissolving in the acid-bath of callous banality. When God's Final Message to His Creation is finally there to be read, even spelling it out one painful letter at a time isn't enough to prolong the hilarious agony for more than a few last pages. There is nothing to do after that end but turn around and become constructive. This is what begins to happen (off-handedly) in the epilogue to *So Long, and Thanks for All the Fish*, which wonders speculatively whether absorption in triviality might, after all, be not so bad as the awesome cosmic vision implies.

Which brings us, as it brought Douglas Adams, to the fundamental interconnectedness of all things.

The bill which Dirk Gently, holistic detective, presents to a client who has hired him to find her cat is still basically bathetic in character, juxtaposing as it does the finding of the cat (deceased) with saving the human race from extinction (for which no charge is made) *via* "Detecting and triangulating vectors of interconnectedness of all things," and a consequent but seemingly-too-convenient trip to the Bahamas. But the absurdity of these juxtapositions is not the same nihilistic absurdity which underlies the Hitch-Hiker books—it is more like an inversion or mirror image of it, not dissimilar in spirit to the Anthropic principle in its confident assertion that contemplation of the apparently trivial may, in fact, be a hotline to the mind-bogglingly important.

The world-view of *Dirk Gently's Holistic Detective Agency* is a much more cheerful one than the world-view of the Hitch-Hiker books, and despite his chaotic lifestyle Dirk Gently is here essentially a winner. An unwary sociologist of literature might put this *bouleversement* down to the simple fact that Douglas Adams had become rich, and hence more contented with his existential lot, but *The Long Dark Tea-Time of the Soul* would prove him wrong, because that book is much closer in tone to the later Hitch-Hiker books, and offers us a rather different Dirk Gently, a rather different universe, and a rather different fundamental interconnectedness of all things.

GALACTIC HITCH-HIKER: DOUGLAS ADAMS

Dirk Gently's Holistic Detective Agency is Douglas Adams's best book, and not just because it is his most cheerful. It has an intricacy which really does bind together the trivial and the apocalyptic, employing the aesthetic elegance of time paradoxes. When the inconsistently-sharp Dirk deduces from a second-hand account of a conjuring trick done to amuse a child the existence of the time-machine and the time-traveller, whose true nature has been efficiently cloaked by academic obscurity, the reader's reaction is one of delight at the closing of an elegant connection. The import of Dirk's own subsequent time-travelling mission is similarly delightful, though unusually esoteric in a book written for a mass audience. Despite these connections, however—and despite the assertion that what is being proved is the fundamental interconnectedness of everything—the supposed holism of Gently's method is a sham.

The Gently books are not really exercises in the detective genre because they are far too subversive of its parameters. Gently will have nothing of the Holmesian dictum that when you have eliminated the impossible, whatever remains, however improbable, must be true. The fact that we regard something as "improbable," he points out, reveals that we have some actual ground for assessing its unlikelihood; to reject something as "impossible" may only mean that it is something we cannot understand. There are, as he dutifully observes, *lots* of things we don't understand.

But the substitution of an holistic attitude for a reductionist one is only momentarily enlivening. Once we accommodate the impossible within our patterns of reasoning, as Gently tries to do (following—despite his declared distaste for them—the many champions of astrology, alternative medicine, and the paranormal), our criteria of investigation become aesthetic rather than logical. We cease to ask whether things make sense, and must ask instead whether they make a neat pattern. In *Dirk Gently's Holistic Detective Agency* they do, but only because they are contrived so to do. In *The Long Dark Tea-Time of the Soul* they don't, because Douglas Adams (who remains a reductionist at heart) can't believe that in the final analysis they really do.

"The long dark tea-time of the soul" is a phrase borrowed from *Life, the Universe and Everything*, where it is used to sum up the existential predicament of the immortal Wowbagger, whose efforts to avoid *ennui* prove ultimately fruitless. In the novel the phrase describes the similar predicament of the immortal gods of Asgard, whose efforts have likewise come to naught—indeed, Odin's attempt to cultivate eternal bliss by calculated obsession with the quality of his bed-linen is suspiciously similar to the tactics of mortals whose attempts to combat *angst* are equally absurd. Adams's imaginative pendulum has swung back again to the outlook of the later and grimmer Hitch-Hiker books, and the fundamental interconnectedness of all things now looks just as bleak and silly as God's Final Message to His Creation. Holism, which briefly seemed in the first novel of the series to have a chance of holiness, turns out to be merely holey. The old gods have nothing at all to say to us, and if there are to be new ones we must look for their origins not to the blazing light of a star shining over Bethlehem, but rather in the unthinkably disgusting mess lurking in a discarded refrigerator. Advent has gone the way of the Apocalypse.

As Raymond Chandler once observed (I paraphrase in the interests of brevity), the unbiased onlooker is bound to conclude that the world is a pretty sick place. In an oft-quoted moment of rebellion Chandler insisted that "Down these mean streets a man must go who is not himself mean...," and he sent Philip Marlowe. Unfortunately (but inevitably) Marlowe's presence didn't make the streets any less mean, and despite his non-meanness he failed conspicuously to avoid the

103

ravages of *angst*. Dirk Gently started off a good deal meaner than Marlowe ever was, and the fact that his mean streets quickly unfolded to reveal a much more complicated system of thoroughfares really didn't help very much. His inevitable regress from potential hero to actual victim has been much more rapid than Marlowe's, and it is difficult to imagine his prospects improving if he is ever entrusted with another case. His future adventures, if any, may be funny, but one cannot escape the suspicion that they might turn out to be funny in exactly the same way as *So Long, and Thanks for All the Fish*—the danger is that they will become nothing more than mordant comedies of ludicrous failure.

It is arguable that the only British humorist who nearly managed to sustain his form over the course of a long career as a novelist was P. G. Wodehouse. The prospect facing anyone who might attempt to emulate Wodehouse is not encouraging, because what Wodehouse did, essentially, was to subvert the pretensions of the upper classes by making them look absurd—and that project kept him in work for such a long time only because the upper classes stubbornly, heroically, and against all logic managed to preserve those pretensions to be further subverted. The anarchic comedians of today have found no order to assault which is anywhere near as resilient; nowadays, subversion is usually too effective for its own good. If anything even looks as if it might become sacred it can be made to look stupid with consummate ease. There is little future in mocking pretentiousness when pretention itself has come to seem little more than a form of self-parody.

This puts humorists like Douglas Adams in a much more difficult predicament than most other writers who have fallen or fought their way into best-seller status. The writer of thud-and-blunder fantasy trilogies can produce more and more of the same, gaining in facility with practice, and can be confident not only of lasting as long as the boom, but of cultivating habits which might be transferable to whichever kind of action adventure next inherits the mantle of fashionability. The literary humorist, alas, must forever be in search of something fresh to enliven his productions.

Unlike the screen humorist, who can in times of stress always fall back on sight gags, confident that slapstick will never lose its appeal, the witty novelist must rely on the world to provide him with a steady stream of new absurdities to expose ("the world," in this context, takes in the scientific world-view and the conventions of literary genres, too). The man who is too adept at this kind of work might easily write himself out of a job. and there is a certain telling paradox in the fact that Douglas Adams, who got to be a bestseller because he is very good at his job, is continually making his job that much harder to do.

The direction in which Adams will probably have to go, if he is to survive as a best-seller writer until it is time to hang up his word-processor and get deeply into bed-linen, is already mapped out in *Dirk Gently's Holistic Detective Agency*, though Gently's own career will have to get out of the doldrums of *The Long Dark Tea-Time of the Soul* if he is going to be Adams's long-term torch-bearer. It is in intricate and intriguing patterns of connection rather than continually crushing revelations of meaninglessness that the prospects of future delight will lie.

His legion of admirers must be hopeful that Douglas Adams may become a more whole-hearted holist than his latest book reveals him yet to be, and that his inventiveness will guide him to pleasant pastures which will not be so quickly blighted by the awfulness of apocalyptic *angst*. If he cannot, a long dark tea-time may be waiting to claim his own artistic soul.

VI.

THE CHRONICLES OF STEPHEN R. DONALDSON

THE FANTASTIST

If Stephen R. Donaldson did not exist, no writer of exemplary fictions would have dared to invent him. Having decided that his vocation was to be a writer, he spent years laboring, without income, on *The Chronicles of Thomas Covenant*. He obtained a list of forty-seven American publishers and began submitting an outline and sample to them, in alphabetical order. Some of them liked it enough to ask to see more, and some talked about the possibility of publishing it—if, and only if, the central character's predicament could be softened. When all forty-seven had rejected it, though, Donaldson simply went back to B and resubmitted it to Ballantine, although he was unaware of the fact that new editorial staff had been made responsible for their fantasy line. Lester del Rey bought and published the trilogy—which, without any appreciable hype, rapidly became a bestseller.

This is a story which can give heart to all would-be writers frustrated by editorial indifference, and it is all to the good that a story which can function so well as a parable should have the weight of indisputable truth upon it (the story of Robert the Bruce and the spider, for example, suffers from a suspicious lightness as well as an unfortunate lack of strict pertinence). It also reveals a truth which is, if you think about it, rather awesome: that the assembled editorial staff of the entire American publishing establishment can be utterly and unanimously wrong in their considered judgment of what the reading public will like and respond to.

Some of the editors who rejected the *Chronicles* were sufficiently interested by what they saw to ask to see more, but not one of the forty-seven could believe that readers would be willing to sympathize with and identify with a leper; about this they were not only wrong but spectacularly wrong. Lester del Rey's apparent courage and perspicacity in leaping this hurdle was soon exposed as a freak, when del Rey objected very strenuously to the alleged unmarketability of a subsequent Donaldson protagonist, on the grounds that she was female. Donaldson, who had firmly resisted pressure to make Thomas Covenant a mere asthmatic even while he was unpublished and unwaged, was inevitably unimpressed by this objection.

We should not be too surprised by the discovery that the supposed wisdom of publishers is mere prejudice; the history of literature is, after all, littered with ready-made sure-fire bestsellers which even hype could not make profitable, and oft-rejected books which eventually sold millions, thanks to word-of-mouth promotion by consumers. Never before, though, had there been a test-case quite as clear and absolute as this one. But when we have had our fill of gloating, we must admit that this mass editorial failure is a puzzling phenomenon. How can it possibly be the case that forty-seven editors (who must be prolific readers themselves) misjudged so completely the likely response of vast numbers of readers?

ALGEBRAIC FANTASIES & REALISTIC ROMANCES, by Brian Stableford

In taking up my allotted task of trying to explain why Stephen Donaldson's books have been so successful I have hindsight on my side. It is always easy to pick the Derby winner on the day after the race, and to identify a dozen good and excellent reasons why that was the horse to bet on; it is equally easy to criticize those who were unfortunate enough to pick the wrong one. But the really interesting questions we must ask about the editors who had not the benefit of hindsight and thus ended up with egg on their collective faces have to do with their reasons for turning down the *Chronicles*, and why they turned out to be wrong. In the failure of those reasons there ought to be a significant revelation about the aims, desires, and accomplishments of the act of reading as practiced by large numbers of people.

The reasons why *Chronicles* was rejected are not, of course, enshrined in any written record, save for the few requests which were made for rewriting (which are known to me only by hearsay). It is, however, not too difficult to identify certain features of the trilogy which presumably led editors to be suspicious of its market potential. Some of them have, in fact, brought complaints from reviewers and have been wittily caricatured by parodists (including Joanna Russ and David Langford).

To start with, Donaldson's use of language might easily have appeared to an editor to be a barrier to the enjoyment of many readers. He uses many unfamiliar words, some of whose meanings would probably be wrongly guessed by the unwary reader. For example, it is difficult to deduce from context that "gelid" means "icy," and I must confess to being rather surprised when I learned that "anile" means "like an old woman," and not what my rough-and-ready etymological instincts suggested to me that might mean when first I encountered it. Nor is Donaldson's use of language simply a matter of deploying a sophisticated vocabulary, for his use of such words as "sojourn," "mien," and "periapt" in both *Chronicles* and *The Second Chronicles of Thomas Covenant* is sometimes rather suspect in its accuracy.

The fact that abstruse vocabulary is a stylistic device which Donaldson has since abandoned—the two-volume *Mordant's Need* is written in a very different manner—gives the impression that it was to some extent an idiosyncrasy born of inexperience, but the intriguing thing is that it not only failed to deter the readers who loved *Chronicles* but—I suspect—may actually have enhanced their appreciation of the work.

There are two arguments which can be used to back up this hypothesis. Firstly, the use of an exotic vocabulary in describing a fantasy world may help to cultivate the sense of difference and magicality which must characterize that world as an entity rather different from our own. Secondly, the need to deploy such terms arises, at least in part, as a corollary of other stylistic features of *Chronicles* and *Second Chronicles*—which are, in terms of describing the feelings of their central characters, uneconomical to the point of excess. It is when a writer feels compelled to hammer home a point by emphatic repetition that he is most inclined to reach for the Thesaurus.

To call Donaldson's prose "uneconomical to the point of excess" may sound pejorative, and there are doubtless some critics who would intend it thus, but we must not overlook the fact that in terms of reader appeal excess can very often be a virtue. Heavy emphasis, including lavish italicization and the liberal use of short sentences and exclamation marks, as well as repetitiveness, can be very effective, once the consent of the reader has been won, in giving a text affective power. When the primary appeal of a text is to the emotions of the reader—as it is, for instance, in genre romantic fiction—this kind of device is frequently successful where no other can be. Subtlety and punctiliousness have by definition a certain coolness which does not lend itself to texts whose determination is to make constant play with the most deep-seated emotions of the reader.

Not all heroic fantasy is emotional in this way, of course, and it is a mistake to assume that all three-decker fantasies are eggs in the same basket. Though subject-matter and marketing technique make comparisons with Tolkien inevitable, Tolkien is a very much cooler and more studied narrator than Donaldson, and Donaldson boldly went where no writer had ever gone before in designing the predicament of his hero to justify his experience of extraordinary pain and hysteria. What the editors who rejected *Chronicles* could not believe was that large numbers of readers would be willing to follow him to such extremes; we now know that they miscalculated.

The mistake is less surprising when we remember that editors are *professional* readers. They read with a clinical eye, their intrinsic relationship with the text very different from that of the everyday reader. Precisely because their reading is informed by theories about what the everyday reader gets out of reading, editors are no longer capable of functioning as everyday readers; they have lost the essential naivety of everyday reading. When they deal with the cool and cerebral aspects of fiction, this probably does not matter much—but when they have to deal with the emotional, gut-grabbing aspects of fiction, it matters a lot. Because an editor's guts are essentially ungrabbable, he is apt to misjudge (catastrophically in the case of *Chronicles*) the gut-grabbing potential of the works which he reads.

The Chronicles of Thomas Covenant and its sequel demonstrated that vast numbers of readers—which means not just habitual fantasy fans but all those other shop assistants and estate agents, factory-workers and taxi-drivers who read only a few books a year—were not only prepared to immerse themselves in the predicament of a man with a particularly horrible disease, but were avid to do so. They were prepared to be absolutely fascinated by that character's translocation into a secondary world whose entire history, geography, and metaphysics reflected that predicament, so that his struggle for survival as a social being became inextricably entwined with the demand that he play savior to an entire world. They were prepared to participate in his quest, which was explicitly stated to be a hard battle against his own unbelief, primarily directed against an enemy which personified the determination of others to *despise* him.

These facts are, in their way, very revealing. It is a long time since Thoreau pointed out, in *Walden*, that "the mass of men lead lives of quiet desperation," and yet it is a lesson which none of us ever quite learns. Each of us is well aware of his or her own desperation, of the extent to which we cannot quite believe in ourselves, of the deep and awful fear which we all have that others think badly of us (with some justification)—but none of us can ever quite believe it of everyone else, because we are fooled by the acts they put on, just as they—notwithstanding our fears—are mostly fooled by ours.

In making his adversary—his Satan, in the literal meaning of the term—a Despiser, Donaldson got down-to the nitty-gritty of our everyday experience of anxiety in a new way; that is why *Chronicles* seemed to so many of its readers to be a revelation, and something which fully deserved their interest and commitment.

Donaldson was not the first writer to use fantasy fiction to display the ills and alienations felt by people in this world as key features of a Secondary World whose "reality" is deliberately made dubious. There are some excellent and meticulous examples to be found in that species of "young adult" fantasy which attempts to speak directly to the unease of adolescents; Catherine Storr's *Marianne Dreams* and William Mayne's *A Game of Dark* are two of them. But the appeal of *Chronicles* was both broader and more ambitious than any which had gone before; its uncompromising deployment of a literal leper was a clarion call to all who fear the metaphorical social leprosy of being not merely disliked, which is bad enough—but *despised*. In so doing, the narrative had to establish its credentials as a book which would not shirk in any way the touching of raw nerves, and with that end in view, its use of excess in style, in language, and in imagery is justified.

There is a ludicrous irony in the fact that Lester del Rey, who bought *Chronicles* when no one else would, then tried to oppose Donaldson's decision to use a female protagonist, on the grounds that heroic fantasy is or should be essentially masculine in character ("It's like writing Tarzan with Jane as the hero," he is rumored to have said). It is highly probable that an important aspect of the runaway success of *Chronicles* was partly due to the fact that it caught the imagination of many female readers, and some of its stylistic devices have much in common with fiction aimed at a strictly female audience. There is a definite propriety, if not a certain inevitability, about the fact that the real protagonist of *Second Chronicles* is Linden Avery, and the fact that when Donaldson began to experiment with a very different narrative voice in the novella, "Daughter of Regals"—which can almost be regarded as a preliminary sketch for *Mordant's Need*—he used a female protagonist.

This propriety does not arise from the fact that Donaldson is carefully courting a female audience (he is far too committed to his mission as a writer to be interested in cynical commercial calculations of that kind), but from the fact that it is far easier to model the kind of existential predicament in which he is most interested by using female characters. We all bring to reading a world-view infused by patriarchal assumptions, which necessitate a male character being stigmatized in some way (leprosy is merely an extreme example) before he can be fully exposed to the force of Despite; females have more than a head start in the everyday business of being despised, feeling guilty, and taking blame, and these characteristics can be easily attached to female characters in stories.

It is significant, in this respect, that Thomas Covenant's relationships with women expose him to the power of Despite in two very different ways. On the one hand, his wife's rejection of him comes to symbolize the world's, but on the other, there is his rape of Lena, the girl who befriends him following his translocation to the Secondary World. At that point in the story he cannot see the Land as anything other than a dream, but rather than constituting an excuse for his action, this simply emphasizes the point at issue: that in our secret dreams, we are capable of a brutality which we not only could not acknowledge publicly, but which we find horrific in ourselves. In *Mordant's Need* we do not need to be told that Terisa is diseased, nor do we need to see her commit some evil act, in order to believe completely in her lack of self-esteem; we only need to be told (and we believe *that* without any conspicuous demonstration) that her rich father is an arrogant and overbearing pig.

It is true that there is much heroic fantasy which is masculine in character, celebrating the joys of *machismo* and the value of lusty barbarism against supposedly-corrupt civility and sensibility; Conan and Tarzan are key examples. Whichever sex his protagonists may be, though, Donaldson's work does not belong to this category. His heroism is of a very different kind, which is fundamentally patient and resilient, becoming active and assertive only occasionally and peculiarly.

Whatever physical power Donaldson's characters have is not only magical, but locked up within them, mysteriously beyond the reach of conscious control; they usually do not believe that they have it, and sometimes (as in "Daughters of Regals") have powerful, if misleading, reasons to believe that they do *not* have it.

Nor, for the most part, do they compensate for their lack of physical power with exceptional cleverness; though they are certainly no fools, they always lack the information necessary to help them reason their way through their predicaments.

Thus, the desperate emotions to which Donaldson's characters are subject not only define their situations, but must be their principal guide—and if the reader is to entertain hope for their eventual success, he or she must pin that hope to the steering power of their fundamental attraction to good and repulsion by evil. The dramatic tension in Donaldson's plots comes from doubt that this will be the case—in Thomas Covenant's case because he knows only too well his own capacity for evil, in Terisa Morgan's case because of her initial sexual attraction to the deceptive Eremis.

Whether one prefers this kind of heroism to the other is a matter of taste, but it is a matter of taste which has distinct moral connotations. The moral weight of Donaldson's fantasies—which is quite inseparable from the manner of their emotional appeal—is the other distinctive feature which needs to be taken into account in attempting to explain the wide popularity of his works.

All fiction has moral weight because the author, in playing the part of providence within his imagined world, cannot help but make moral decisions as to which of his characters will be rewarded and which will suffer. Secondary World fantasy exaggerates this by dealing with hypothetical worlds which are overtly and intrinsically morally ordered; providence enters into the landscape as an animistic force, so that good and evil are everywhere immanent, waiting only to be triggered by the magic potential inherent in the characters.

On first consideration, the fact that Thomas Covenant cannot consciously command his own magical power may seem to make him incapable of moral action—he must stand by, raging helplessly, while evil is done which he does not know how to prevent; and when the white tornado finally does erupt from his ring he is as helpless to direct it as those who suffer its wrath. In fact, though, it would be dodging the real issue to put a fantasy hero in complete control of his magic potential, because the question of who we would snuff out of existence if we only had the magic power to do it is neither an interesting nor a pertinent moral question. A far more interesting question is how we might conduct ourselves in a universe in which, despite an acknowledged and intrinsic moral order, good seems to be losing out to evil. In such a universe one must have hope in the eventual triumph of good—one of the best lessons of fantasy fiction is that hope is far more dependable than orthodox faith—but one must also accept responsibility for the promotion of that hope.

Whether or not the battles which are fought in the imaginative arena of fantasy fiction have any relevance for the grand stage of our own universe is very dubious, despite attempts by the faithful to preserve hope that our world too has an interested and morally-responsible Creator—but of their relevance to the personal life of the individual, lived within the private universe of the ego, there can be no doubt. We are all authors constantly about the business of constructing the narratives of our own lives (our life-stories) and responsibility for the maintenance of hope and self-esteem cannot be shirked—not, at any rate, without the most grievous danger to our *morale*.

When Stephen Donaldson asks for our sympathy for the all-too-frail Thomas Covenant, or begs us to hope that Linden Avery will find deliverance from her undeserved guilt, or invites us to join Terisa Morgan in her attempts to penetrate an astonishingly complicated web of intrigue and illusion, we are being asked a serious question. And what we might possibly get out of these books (and others of their kind) is a burst of good feeling which can leave a useful legacy within us. It really does matter what kind of heroes are offered by our fantasies, and whether one sort is better than another.

Donaldson, though he is the son of a missionary, is not usually an overt preacher—his dissent from the message of traditional preachers is made abundantly clear by a hard-hitting chapter in Volume Three of *Chronicles*, ironically entitled "The Danger of Dreams," and by his novella, "Ser Visal's Tale"—but he is a writer steadfastly and unrepentantly aligned with the angels. There is a very revealing remark in the introduction to "Daughter of Regals," where he refers to a story which was written for an anthology of "religious fantasy"—and which features a Covenantesque angel—as being "a bit more overt than usual." Elsewhere in the same collection, most especially in the effectively horrific "The Conqueror Worm," the moral weight of his fantasy is deeply-buried, but it remains the heart and soul of what he does. That is another thing which the hard-headed editors of America overlooked when they deemed *Chronicles* unsuitable for publication: the resentment which many people have when they are preached at is symptomatic of a resistance to moral tyranny which has mercifully become common in the West; it is *not* a refusal to be interested in moral questions.

Donaldson is on record as having said that he "distrusts the word allegory," but that is because he has doubts about how broad the traditionally-narrow definition of allegory might sensibly be made. Certainly he has characters who stand for qualities, and his choice of proper names often calls forth significant resonances—significant examples include his use of the name Elohim in *Second Chronicles*, and his attachment of the name Orison to the city/citadel of *Mordant's Need*. However loose and partial the allegorical aspects of his work are, they are important, and it is significant for those readers who have followed his career thus far that he has not stood still in terms of his own moral sensibilities—compare, for instance, the definition of Thomas Covenant's predicament in *Chronicles* (and thus the nature of the victory spelled out in the last line) with the climactic events of *Second Chronicles*. Donaldson is an explorer, not a ritualist, and in appreciating that, his public is yet another step ahead of what the contemptuous editors of America conventionally expect from the audience they serve.

Stephen R. Donaldson belongs to that rare breed of writer whose members spring to fame at a single bound (which is by no means the same as being an overnight success, as those long years of unwaged labor remind us). He did not make concessions to the vagaries of market demand before making that leap, and it would be ridiculous to expect him to make any in future. His writing is an authentic vocation, but he knows very well that writing is a kind of communication, and he does not do it to flatter his own idiosyncrasies, but in the hope and expectation of grabbing a few guts. It is highly unlikely that following his own inclinations will lead him to forsake the rapport which he has with his readers.

The fact that *The Second Chronicles of Thomas Covenant* and *Mordant's Need* are single coherent narratives despite having to be carved up into smaller units for publication demonstrates that Donaldson is comfortable working at the protracted length at which modern fantasies seem to work best. Although *Second Chronicles*, like the authentic trilogy to which it was a sequel, uses well-tried means to acquire great length—the constant movement of the characters from one locale to another and their frequent interruption and delay by opposing forces—*Mordant's Need* is striking in maintaining a narrative of great intricacy, set in a single location, for nearly three-quarters of its total length (which is well over half a million words). This accomplishment should not be underestimated, and promises that Donaldson has abundant scope for making progress in his work. We have yet to see how far his range as a writer may be extended (and this article has left aside his excursion into the mystery story), but he is still a relatively young man, and there is no reason why his creativity and exploratory verve should give out for many years to come.

VII.

ANIMAL SPIRITS

THE EROTIC AND THE SUPERNATURAL
IN MICHAEL JACKSON'S "THRILLER" VIDEO

Michael Jackson's *Thriller* video, co-written by Jackson and John Landis and directed by Landis, is both an instance of and a commentary on the changing implications of erotic symbolism in supernatural fiction. It is, in a way, a celebration of the fact that what were once covert meanings have risen to the level of consciousness, permitting modern supernatural fiction a depth of ironic reflection which has some interesting consequences. One of those consequences is that while the technology of cinematic special effects has become more sophisticated, permitting the imagery of horror films to become much more gruesome, the films have actually become less frightening, and have in fact moved almost into the category of black comedy. The *Thriller* video, which co-opts all the tricks of contemporary make-up artistry to stunning effect, awoke sufficient disquiet among American Fundamentalist moralists to call forth a quasi-apologetic disclaimer from Michael Jackson; but in fact the video subverts its own imagery very efficiently, and the net effect is to delight rather than to terrify. Because it is *self-consciously* nightmarish it is a story *about* nightmares, not a nightmare in itself, and what it says about nightmares is partly a decoding of their nature and symbology.

The story told in the video has three distinct phases. Phase one begins with a car rolling to a halt on a country road. It contains a boy (played by Michael Jackson) and a girl. The boy tells the girl, uncertainly, that the car seems to have run out of gas. She does not question this, though she obviously knows it for the *clichéd* pretext that it is. The two go for a walk in the dark, and the boy raises the question of their feelings for one another; with her tacit encouragement he asks her to be "his girl." She gratefully accepts this offer, and in the course of a tender embrace he gives her a ring. Then he says that he is "not like other guys." This is a joke for the audience to share, because we know that she will take the wrong inference from the remark. She thinks he is simply trying to convince her of the seriousness of his affections, but we, already wise in the ways of cinematic convention, know that he is actually implying something more sinister. So far, the girl has been entirely correct in "reading" the covert meanings within the boy's courtship maneuvers, and she is being entirely consistent in interpreting this one the way she does—but we in the audience are quite aware that a crucial shift of interpretative framework is taking place. The shift is symbolically signalled by a shot of clouds moving away to expose the face of the full moon, and then the boy begins to turn into that curious kind of humanoid wolf which has been—since Stuart Walker's 1935 film, *The Werewolf of London*—the cinema's stereotype of lycanthropic transformation.

When the girl catches up with the audience in realizing that she is in a new kind of situation, she reacts in the manner which countless old movies have established as a stock response: she starts screaming and runs away. The boy, at first, urges her to run (confirming that, in this stereotype, the werewolf is a rather tragic figure—the unwilling but helpless victim of his condition). Once the transformation is complete, though, his bestial self obliterates both conscience and consciousness, and he chases her.

At this point, phase one fades out into phase two, becoming only an image on a cinema screen that is being watched by a boy (played by Michael Jackson) and a girl (played by the actress who played the girl in phase one). Their clothes and hairstyles are quite different now, much more in tune with current fashion, suggesting a marked time difference between the two sets of images. This reminds us that phase one reflected the imagery of 1950s low-budget teenage scare-movies (the archetype of the species being, of course, Gene Fowler's *I Was a Teenage Werewolf*, made in 1957).

The reactions of the watching boy and girl are quite different. The girl is repelled by what she is watching, and seems to be finding it hard to bear, but the boy is obviously enjoying himself, seemingly enthralled while he wolfs popcorn with unthinking relish. (The obvious symbolic propriety of the popcorn and the relish with which it is being consumed is unlikely to be accidental.) The girl leaves the cinema, and the boy reluctantly follows. He tells her, with an element of contempt in his reassurance, that it was only a film; she replies resentfully that "It's not funny." He charges her with being afraid, and her denial—though obviously false—does serve to emphasize that fear is not the only matter at issue. The display that has so fascinated *him,* she has found repulsive. The boy at this point assumes a protective role, assuring her that he will see her safely home.

It is while they walk through the dark streets that Jackson begins to sing. Here we have another change of interpretative framework—the transference made conventional by countless musicals, which allow the play and its performers to move smoothly out of a "naturalistic" mode of presentation into a highly-stylized one. Audiences have long since given tacit permission for this kind of transference to be very extreme indeed—the cardinal examples being found in such movies as Mervyn LeRoy's *Gold Diggers of 1933*, whose story-line about dancers struggling to get by in the Depression is seamlessly juxtaposed with Busby Berkeley's fabulous musical set-pieces.

Until he starts to sing Michael Jackson is an *actor* in the video, playing the parts of ordinary adolescents trying to make out with their girl-friends, but once he starts to sing the context shifts according to the convention. It is an interesting paradox that it is when the story shifts from the naturalistic to the fantastic mode that he stops pretending and becomes himself. The lyrics of the song, of course, relate explicitly to the mundane storyline. The title and keyword is first made to refer to the kind of film which the boy and girl have been watching. and to the effects of such a film on its watchers. The hypothetical "I" of the lyric (to be distinguished from the performer) claims the role which the boy assumed in protectively offering to see the girl home, guarding her against the phantoms of her imagination. The fact that he is willing and able to do this is credited to his accepted affection for her (the point is made even more deftly in the lyric of another recent hit, "The Power of Love" by Frankie Goes to Hollywood, which includes the reverently-crooned lines, "I'll protect you from the Hooded Claw/Keep the vampires from your door.")

At this stage, however, Jackson completes only part of the song, because the lyric itself is going to undergo a transformation, offering us in its latter part a different set of meanings for its title and keyword. In the video, Jackson reverts to the part of the boy, but the interpretative context of the film does not revert all the way back to the naturalistic. We are still in a fantasized mode, and this is signalled to us by the sound-track, which supplements the pictures with a short poem read by the actor Vincent Price, in the marvellous camp-horror style which he made famous in such films as Roger Corman's *The Raven* (1963) and Robert Fuest's *The Abominable Dr. Phibes* (1971). (When the boy and girl emerged from the cinema the lighted advertisement above the entrance claimed that Vincent Price was starring in a film called *Thriller*.)

As the poem proceeds the images on the screen are once again taken over by the iconography of the horror film, but this time the films whose imagery is being coopted belong to a more recent and more visceral tradition begun by George Romero's *Night of the Living Dead* (1968). Rotting corpses emerge from their graves and from the sewers beneath the streets, congregating into a ghoulish and threatening company. The boy and girl now seem equally afraid, but when the girl turns to the boy for the protection which he promised her, he again begins a transformation. This is a more complicated shift of mode within the film, because the boy-into-ghoul change is coupled with the actor-into-performer switch as the singing begins again. Now Jackson and the ghouls embark upon a stagy dance-routine—a change of behavior which is sanctioned by the conventions of movie musicals, and which is just as smooth as the first eruption of song. The import of the lyric is now quite different, with the hypothetical singer promising the addressee of the song that he can provide her with a bigger thrill than any horror film if she will let him make love to her. While the hypothetical singer is making this rather extravagant promise the actual singer, Jackson, is made up to look like a pseudo-Karloffian monster, leading a dozen other such monsters in disco-style programmed cavorting.

The choreography of this section of the video requires the girl to put on a show of trying to escape her "pursuers," but it is only when the song ends and the context reverts again to the more commonplace fantastic mode that she runs indoors and tries to barricade herself into her room. The barricading is ineffectual, as monsters begin smashing their way through a shuttered window and up through the splintering floorboards. The boy-ghoul strides implacably through the shattering door to embrace her.

At this point, phase two of the story gives way to phase three. Just as the first point of transition relegated the substance of phase one to the level of "harmless fantasy," so the second relegates phase two. This time, the recourse is to the hoariest of all literary and cinematic *clichés*, reducing the horrific experience to the status of a dream. Instead of the boy-ghoul reaching out for the girl, we now have only the boy; it is light instead of dark, and the filthy, empty room has become a cosy furnished one. The boy tells the girl that she has been dreaming, and he soothingly assumes the protective role again, promising her as he did in phase two to see her home. The girl accepts this, but the audience is again expected to be one step ahead of her—the climactic moment when the boy, as he guides her towards the door, half-turns to the camera to reveal yellow, slit-pupilled eyes (the same eyes he wore as a wolf man) is a confirmation as much as a surprise. The constant moves from "fantasy" into "reality" are, we are assured, nothing of the kind. The abandonment of a particular set of symbols does not allow us to escape or set aside that which is being symbolized.

The form of the storyline which Jackson and Landis use in the *Thriller* video has several literary precedents, ranging from Jan Potocki's *The Saragossa Manuscript* (1804) to Robert Irwin's *The Arabian Nightmare* (1983). The idea of a series of apparent returns from fantasy to reality, all of which ultimately prove to be nothing of the kind, is extensively deployed by Philip K. Dick in numerous novels, including *Eye in the Sky* (1957), *The Three Stigmata of Palmer Eldritch*, (1964) and *Now Wait for Last Year* (1966). All these literary works, though, are asking questions which are metaphysical in character; they attempt to cultivate a sense of existential unease by challenging the idea that we can readily identify what is real. In the *Thriller* video this is not so much the end as the means of raising a further series of questions about the relationship between our fantasies and our feelings.

Underlying the symbology of the *Thriller* video and the other horror films to which it refers is the very old idea that human nature is in an important sense *divided*, and that our powers of reason and moral conscience are engaged in an ongoing war with more bestial impulses and passions. For Plato the human soul was pure reason, but when embodied it became embroiled with mortal and irrational elements: a "spirited part" of nobler aspirations like ambition and the love of power, and "lower appetites" that should, ideally, be annihilated by the force of the will. The Stoics considered the passions to be perturbations and diseases of the mind, overpowering impulses contrary to nature and insubordinate to reason. In a later era, the rationalist philosopher Spinoza founded his ethical theories in the proposition that "Our mind acts certain things and suffers others," proceeding to offer one discourse "On human servitude, or the Strength of the Emotions" and another "Concerning the power of the intellect, or Human Freedom." Descartes, in his similar philosophical system, represented the passions as excitations of the soul caused by the movement of "animal spirits." In a more scientific era Darwin, in his book on *The Expression of the Emotions in Man and Animals*, conceded that our emotional responses are atavistic, innate, and in the final analysis uncontrollable by the power of the will. Freud imagined the essential self—the *ego*—developing as a result of the dialectical contention of the moral and rational *superego* and the anarchic, thrustful *id*.

In view of the fact that this is the way we experience our inner life, it is hardly surprising to find in myth and supernatural literature exaggerated images of divided man: stories in which the fragile grip of reason is broken down by the awful force of animal passion. This is why we can "understand" such non-existent beings as werewolves, and why we are so fascinated by the plight of Dr. Jekyll in Stevenson's brilliant nightmare-based fantasy, *Dr. Jekyll and Mr. Hyde*, the basis of three of the best horror films ever made. It is significant that the film versions of *Jekyll and Hyde* are all much less coy than Stevenson in giving Hyde's evil a specifically sexual context, because it is in the area of sexual relationships that we are most likely to encounter the irresistible influence of "the passions." In modern parlance, of course, "passion" is almost invariably used in a sexual sense, to signify lust and jealousy.

There have been individuals, like Plato and various adherents of Victorian morality, who have regarded the "baser" part of man's nature as an unmitigated evil, to be ruthlessly suppressed; but the vast majority have always had mixed feelings about it. We can see, and regret, certain destructive aspects of the dominion of passion (this is what underlies the modern sense of tragedy), but we find the image of the paragon of reason and unshakable morality a rather horrible one. We find it impossible to be wholeheartedly ashamed of our lusts, and it is from the experience of passion that we derive our moments of intensest pleasure and our occasional ecstatic conviction of the worth of existence. Even the most high-minded of intellectuals is aware of this—it was not the force of pure reason that made Archimedes leap from his bath crying, "Eureka!"

Just as we tend to see human nature in the broad sense as something "divided"—a unity of conflicting forces—so we tend to see sexual love as an almost paradoxical confusion of impulses. The lover intends to be caring, protective, and sensitive, but these intentions are in dialectical opposition to the urges of physical lust which aim toward ends that seem (in the moral context superimposed by our social codes) to amount to violation of the female by the male.

This is what the sexual subtext of the *Thriller* video is all about. In each of the three phases of the story the boy overtly represents his affection for the girl in terms of protectiveness. In phase one, which looks back to the attitudes of a generation ago, his shyness and hesitancy imply a kind of reverence. This is how the girl "misunderstands" his claim not to be like other guys—she takes him to be affirming adherence to the mythology of the day, according to which, because he really loves her, his carefully running out of gas in a remote spot is not simply a standard ploy in routine seduction. That he *does* subscribe, at least partly, to the idea that if he really loves her he will "respect" her and refrain from pressuring her into having sex, is suggested by his despairing instruction to her to get away as he begins to change. The transformation represents, in symbolic form, the hollowness of the mythology—his shyness and his protectiveness are masks concealing the force within him of the Cartesian "animal spirits," the idea of whose possible release easily lends itself to representation in terms of nice boy becoming ravening beast.

The changed clothes and manner of the characters in phase two emphasize that in the course of the last thirty years we have become more sophisticated in sexual matters. The mores and mythologies of the 1950s now seem quaintly hollow to us. The implied reverence is gone, and instead the boy is impatient with the girl's inability to take pleasure from the film. She is herself rather ashamed of the fact that she is frightened and repelled by the imagery—as a member of the audience she is assumed to have been one step ahead of the girl in the film, able to appreciate the humor of her misunderstanding. Basically though, nothing has changed. The boy is again representing his feelings for the girl mainly in terms of protectiveness, and this is still a mask, which will be symbolically stripped away by a new infusion of "animal spirits" in unhuman form.

Because this is the 1980s and not the 1950s, we do not expect that the boy's courtship of the girl will be respectfully unsullied by actual sexual contact. The assumption of premarital virginity has been set aside, not merely as a folly, but also as a hypocritical misrepresentation of the way things actually were. The fact that sex is no longer to be seen as spoliation—as the proverbial "fate worse than death"—does not, however, mean that the opposition of protectiveness and lust has been fully reconciled, and the second phase of the story makes this clear. The lyric of the song *promises* such a reconciliation, by equating the excitation of fear with the excitation of sexual congress, and promising that the former will be overwhelmed by the latter; but the way that the song is integrated into the story subverts that message. The lyric is split into two distinct parts, dividing the protective representations from the libidinous ones in a perfectly literal way; and in between the two bursts of song the appearance and environment of the singer are dramatically transformed. The girl's "natural" reaction is still to run away, screaming, to try to secure herself against a violation which, in this phase of the video, is actually represented. The third phase is not shifted in time, arising as a movement from dream to waking rather than film to reality; what it implies is that it is only in the private world of her dreams that the girl sees things in this way and gives way to her anxieties—in the "real world" she suppresses the fear-reaction and the idea of violation and is content to appear to accept that the boy's caring protectiveness is not compromised by the animal spirits which, symbolized by the werewolf eyes, still move within him.

117

ALGEBRAIC FANTASIES & REALISTIC ROMANCES, by Brian Stableford

The contrast between old and new attitudes which is displayed in the video is achieved cleverly and self-consciously. While the horror films of the 1950s tacitly assumed a naive audience unaware that the story could be decoded to reveal a sexual subtext (though the script-writers were certainly aware of it), Landis clearly assumes that his audience knows about the patterns of sexual symbolism that he will be deploying. This enables him to "replay" scenes from old horror movies in the knowledge that they will be seen differently, with ironic depth. (He does much the same thing in his revisitation of the wolf man theme in *An American Werewolf in London*.) The sexual subtext of the naive horror movie becomes an ironic joke in the *Thriller* video, although the song "Thriller," taken in isolation, is in its own way just as naively straightforward as the films. The joke, in addition, has a subtext of its own, of which the audience is expected to be just as conscious as the "exposed" subtext of phase one.

What this second subtext points out, in essence, is an important shift in sexual politics that has taken place in the last thirty years or so. In the forties, it was the male lover who was considered to have a "predicament" in respect of the conflicting nature of sexual feelings. *He* was the one who, in the evocative words of the most famous werewolf, George Waggner's *The Wolf Man* (1941), walked a "thorny path" through "no fault of his own." It was he who was in danger of "violating" the person he was supposed to "revere." The female lover was imagined to have a much easier time of it, because it is much easier to reconcile tender feelings of care and concern with *being violated* than it is to be at once protective and threatening. It was tacitly assumed then that when a girl made love she was not necessarily pandering to her own animal spirits, but graciously granting a permission to her lover. In the eighties, by contrast, the situation is more confused. Once it is accepted that sexual intercourse is *not* a matter of violation, but rather a natural part of an intimate relationship, the male is no longer in such a contradictory situation. The dialectical opposition between intention and impulse is not destroyed, but the conflict is nowhere near as fierce. The male of the eighties, as represented by the boy in phase two of the video, can much more readily accept in himself a combination of protective and lustful feelings. The pulling of the thorn from his predicament. though, is paralleled by the intrusion of a more painful dilemma into the situation of the female. She now finds that the burden of moral conflict has been largely transferred to her. Now that she is no longer simply permitting herself to be violated, she can no longer get off the hook of reconciling calculation with impulse. This is clearly displayed in the video story, initially by her embarrassment after leaving the cinema, and ultimately by the narrative transition that relegates her fearful flight from threatened violation to the "safety" of private experience.

The song "Thriller" and the *Thriller* video are both "about" the relationships that exist between fear and sex, but they are "about" it in rather different ways. The song reminds us that fear is a stimulant, that it excites us and that it can enliven our experience; it points out that this is why we find horror films ("thrillers") pleasurable. It goes on to suggest, though, that the thrill to be got from watching horror films is pretty feeble by comparison with the thrill that can be obtained from aspects of real existence—specifically (if we leave the euphemisms aside) from orgasm. The video, by contrast, takes a different course. It reminds us in the first instance that sex is, among other things, an anxious business which has its fearful aspect. It reminds us also that this fearful aspect of sex, which arises partly from the conflict of impulse and morality, lends itself very readily to representation in the symbology of horror fiction, and that horror films exploit this anxiety along with all the other anxieties they exploit. This line of argument leads in a direction quite different from that of the song, concluding with the slightly ghoulish suggestion that our sexual relationships cannot be freed from the infection of this anxiety, and that they are, in fact, corrupted or spoiled by it, at least to some extent. While it is, in its fashion, illustrating the song, the video is also, in its fashion, subverting its message.

The *Thriller* video is a remarkable piece of work for several reasons. Its psychological ingenuity is intimately connected with its technical ingenuity. It contains an astonishing profusion of modes of fictional representation: film, dream, story, song, verse; and it makes elaborate use of conventions associated with two distinct kinds of cinematic discourse in order to fuse them together in seamless continuity. No consideration of the layering of meanings which is achieved by this complex interweaving of representations should overlook the fact that the video belongs to its own distinct mode of representation. We should not lose sight of the fact that although it borrows so heavily from the conventions of film, it is *not* a film itself, but a promotional video for a popular song. In many ways, of course, it is very *like* a film (albeit a short one), but there is one more observation we need to make about the way it relates to its assumed audience. As well as all the other things it is, it is a celebration of Michael Jackson's superstardom—it is, indeed, part of the apparatus of that superstardom. It is not irrelevant that it is he, and not some virtual unknown, who sings the lyric of "Thriller." In normal circumstances, an actor is someone ordinary who is pretending to be someone exceptional, but when Michael Jackson acts the parts of the boys in the video, he is doing exactly the opposite. When he stops acting and starts singing, it is almost as though he is Superman having cast aside his Clark Kent disguise. One corollary of this is that although the hypothetical singer of the lyric might well have trouble convincing the hypothetical addressee that he can give her a bigger thrill than any lousy horror film, Michael Jackson addressing the legions of his fans (which he does simply by singing—his medium is his message) is in a very different situation.

Michael Jackson invites description as a "divided man" in a way rather different from that in which (we have suggested) all men see themselves as divided. He is divided into a seemingly fragile and gentle real individual and a public image of awesome proportions. There can be no sharper contrast than between the tremulous boy of phase one of the video's storyline and the Michael Jackson who finds the sexual fantasies of thousands of adolescent girls focussing upon the fiction of his image. If, while watching the video, we can stand back a little further from the customary assumptions which surround our role as members of an audience, we will remember this fact also, and we will appreciate that there are even more ironies buried within this curious work of art than show up under the microscope of an initial decoding.

NOTES

CHAPTER ONE

1. All quotations without page references are taken from personal correspondence.
2. *Artifex; or, the Future of Craftsmanship*, by John Gloag. London: Kegan Paul, Trench, Trübner & Co., 1926, p. 7-8.
3. *Ibid.*, p. 11.
4. *Tomorrow's Yesterday*, by John Gloag. London: George Allen & Unwin, 1932, p. 143.
5. *The New Pleasure*, by John Gloag. London: George Allen & Unwin, 1933, p. 303.
6. *Winter's Youth*, by John Gloag. London: George Allen & Unwin, 1934, p. 188-189.
7. *Ibid.*, p. 269-270.
8. *Sacred Edifice*, by John Gloag. London: Cassell & Co., 1937, p. 286-287.
9. *Manna*, by John Gloag. London: Cassell & Co., 1940, p. 276-278.
10. *Ibid.*, p. 280.
11. *99%*, by John Gloag. London: Cassell & Co., 1944, p. 166-167.
12. *Ibid.*, p. 168.
13. *First One and Twenty*, by John Gloag. London: George Allen & Unwin, 1946, p. vii.
14. *Ibid.*
15. *Ibid.*, p. viii.

CHAPTER TWO

1. "The Profession of Science Fiction XI: Escape to Infinity," by Bob Shaw, in *Foundation* 10 (June 1976): 15.
2. *Ibid.*, p. 16.
3. *Ibid.*, p. 16-17.
4. *Vertigo*, by Bob Shaw. London: Victor Gollancz, 1978, p. 68-69.
5. *Ibid.*

CHAPTER THREE

1. "In the Year Ten Thousand," from *Songs of Doubt and Dream*, by Edgar Fawcett. New York: Funk & Wagnalls, 1891, p. 57-60.
2. *Douglas Duane*, by Edgar Fawcett, in *Lippincott's Monthly Magazine* (April 1887): 548.
3. *Ibid.*, p. 550.

4. *Ibid.*, p. 615-616. The ellipses are all Fawcett's and do not represent unquoted phrases.
5. *Solarion*, by Edgar Fawcett, in *Lippincott's Monthly Magazine* (September 1889): 320-321.
6. *Ibid.*, p. 338-339.
7. *Ibid.*, p. 340.
8. *Ibid.*, p. 344.
9. *The New Nero*, by Edgar Fawcett. New York: P. F. Collier & Son, "Once a Week Library," 1893, p. 17.
10. *Ibid.*, p. 18-19.
11. *Ibid.*, p. 20.
12. *Ibid.*, p. 58.
13. *Ibid.*, p. 288.
14. *The Ghost of Guy Thyrle*, by Edgar Fawcett. London: Ward Lock & Co., 1895, p. 62-63.
15. *Ibid.*, p. 180-181.
16. *Ibid.*, p. 252.

CHAPTER FOUR

1. *Science, Life, and Literature*, by M. P. Shiel, edited by John Gawsworth. London: Williams & Norgate, 1950, p. 58-60.
2. *The Yellow Danger*, by M. P. Shiel. London: Grant Richards, 1898, p. 12.
3. *Explorers of the Infinite*, by Sam Moskowitz. Cleveland, OH: World Publishing Co., 1963, p. 146.
4. *Ibid.*, p. 148.
5. *The Lord of the Sea*, by M. P. Shiel. New York: Frederick A. Stokes, 1901, p. 338.
6. *The Lord of the Sea*, by M. P. Shiel. London: Victor Gollancz, 1929, p. 209.
7. *Ibid.*, p. 316.
8. *The Purple Cloud*, by M. P. Shiel. Cleveland, OH: World Publishing Co., 1946, p. 202.
9. *The Last Miracle*, by M. P. Shiel. London: Victor Gollancz, 1929, p. 274-275.
10. *Ibid.*, p. 280-281.
11. *This Knot of Life*, by M. P. Shiel. London: Everett & Co., 1909, p. 38-39.
12. *The Yellow Peril*, by M. P. Shiel. London: Victor Gollancz, 1929, p. 324-325.
13. *Science, Life, and Literature*, p. 26.
14. *The Young Men Are Coming*, by M. P. Shiel. London: Victor Gollancz, 1979, p. 88-89.

BIBLIOGRAPHY

Adams, Douglas. *Dirk Gently's Holistic Detective Agency*. New York: Simon & Schuster, 1987. DIRK GENTLY #1.
_____. *The Hitch Hiker's Guide to the Galaxy*. London: Pan Books, 1979. HITCH-HIKER SERIES #1.
_____. *Life, the Universe, and Everything*. London: Pan Books, 1982. HITCH-HIKER SERIES #3.
_____. *The Long Dark Tea-Time of the Soul*. London: Heinemann, 1988. DIRK GENTLY #2.
_____. *The Restaurant at the End of the Universe*. London: Pan Books, 1980. HITCH-HIKER SERIES #2.
_____. *So Long, and Thanks for All the Fish*. London: Pan Books, 1984. HITCH-HIKER SERIES #4.
Coad, Oral Sumner. "Edgar Fawcett," in *The Dictionary of American Biography*. New York: Charles Scribner's Sons, 1931.
Donaldson, Stephen R. *Daughter of Regals, and Other Tales*. New York: A Del Rey Book, Ballantine Books, 1984.
_____. *The Illearth War*. New York: Holt, Rinehart & Winston, 1977. THE CHRONICLES OF THOMAS COVENANT THE UNBELIEVER #2.
_____. *Lord Foul's Bane*. New York: Holt, Rinehart & Winston, 1977. THE CHRONICLES OF THOMAS COVENANT THE UNBELIEVER #1.
_____. *A Man Rides Through*. New York: A Del Rey Book, Ballantine Books, 1987. MORDANT'S NEED #2.
_____. *The Mirror of Her Dreams*. London: Collins, 1986. MORDANT'S NEED #1.
_____. *The One Tree*. New York: A Del Rey Book, Ballantine Books, 1982. THE SECOND CHRONICLES OF THOMAS COVENANT THE UNBELIEVER #2.
_____. *The Power That Preserves*. New York: Holt, Rinehart & Winston, 1977. THE CHRONICLES OF THOMAS COVENANT THE UNBELIEVER #3.
_____. *White Gold Wielder*. New York: A Del Rey Book, Ballantine Books, 1983. THE SECOND CHRONICLES OF THOMAS COVENANT THE UNBELIEVER #3.
_____. *The Wounded Land*. New York: A Del Rey Book, Ballantine Books, 1980. THE SECOND CHRONICLES OF THOMAS COVENANT THE UNBELIEVER #1.
Fawcett, Edgar. *Douglas Duane*, in *Lippincott's Monthly Magazine* (April 1887): 521-631.
_____. *Fantasy and Passion*. Boston: Roberts Brothers, 1878.
_____. *The Ghost of Guy Thyrle*. London: Ward Lock & Co., 1895.
_____. *The New Nero*. New York: P. F. Collier & Son, "Once a Week Library," 1893.
_____. *A Romance of Two Brothers*. New York: Minerva Publishing Co., 1891.
_____. *Solarion*, in *Lippincott's Monthly Magazine* (September 1889): 297-369.
_____. *Songs of Doubt and Dream*. New York: Funk & Wagnalls, 1891.
Gloag, John. *Artifex; or. the Future of Craftsmanship*. London: Kegan Paul, Trench, Trübner & Co., 1926.

_____. *First One and Twenty*. London: George Allen & Unwin, 1946.
_____. *It Makes a Nice Change*. London: Nicholson & Watson Ltd., 1938.
_____. *Manna*. London: Cassell & Co., 1940.
_____. *The New Pleasure*. London: George Allen & Unwin, 1933.
_____. *99%*. London: Cassell & Co., 1944.
_____. *Sacred Edifice*. London: Cassell & Co., 1937.
_____. *Slow*. London: Cassell & Co., 1954.
_____. *Take One a Week*. London: Chantry Publications, 1950.
_____. *Tomorrow's Yesterday*. London: George Allen & Unwin, 1932.
_____. *Winter's Youth*. London: George Allen & Unwin, 1934.
Harrison, Stanley R. *Edgar Fawcett*. Boston: Twayne Publishers, 1972.
Morse, A. Reynolds. *The Works of M. P. Shiel*. Los Angeles, CA: Fantasy Publishing Co., Inc., 1948.
Moskowitz, Sam. *Explorers of the Infinite*. Cleveland, OH: World Publishing Co., 1963.
Shaw, Bob. *The Ceres Solution*. London: Victor Gollancz, 1981.
_____. *Cosmic Kaleidoscope*. London: Victor Gollancz, 1976.
_____. *Ground Zero Man*. New York: Avon, 1971.
_____. *Medusa's Children*. London: Victor Gollancz, 1977.
_____. *Nightwalk*. New York: Banner Books, 1967.
_____. *One Million Tomorrows*. New York: Ace Books, 1970.
_____. *Orbitsville*. London: Victor Gollancz, 1975.
_____. *Other Eyes, Other Days*. London: Victor Gollancz, 1972.
_____. *The Palace of Eternity*. New York: Ace Books, 1969.
_____. "The Profession of Science Fiction XI: Escape to Infinity," in *Foundation* 10 (June 1976).
_____. *Shadow of Heaven*. New York: Avon, 1969.
_____. *Ship of Strangers*. London: Victor Gollancz, 1978.
_____. *Tomorrow Lies in Ambush*. London: Victor Gollancz, 1973.
_____. *The Two-Timers*. New York: Ace Books, 1968.
_____. *Vertigo*. London: Victor Gollancz, 1978.
_____. *Who Goes Here?* London: Victor Gollancz, 1977.
_____. *A Wreath of Stars*. London: Victor Gollancz, 1976.
Shiel, M. P. *Children of the Wind*. London: Grant Richards, 1923.
_____. *Dr. Krasinski's Secret*. New York: Vanguard Press, 1929.
_____. *The Dragon*. London: Grant Richards, 1913.
_____. *How the Old Woman Got Home*. New York: Vanguard Press, 1928.
_____. *The Isle of Lies*. London: Victor Gollancz, 1964.
_____. *The Last Miracle*. London: Victor Gollancz, 1929.
_____. *The Lord of the Sea*. New York: Frederick A. Stokes, 1901.
_____. *The Lord of the Sea*. London: Victor Gollancz, 1929.
_____. *The Purple Cloud*. Cleveland, OH: World Publishing Co., 1946.
_____. *Science, Life, and Literature*, edited by John Gawsworth. London: Williams & Norgate, 1950.
_____. *This Knot of Life*. London: Everett & Co., 1909.
_____. *The Yellow Danger*. London: Grant Richards, 1898.
_____. *The Yellow Peril* (revised version of *The Dragon*). London: Victor Gollancz, 1929.
_____. *The Young Men Are Coming*. London: Victor Gollancz, 1979.

INDEX

www.ingramcontent.com/pod-product-compliance
Lightning Source LLC
La Vergne TN
LVHW011359080426
835511LV00005B/347